JAN 2014

WITHDRAWN

Your

NEW JERSEY

WILLS, TRUSTS, & ESTATES
EXPLAINED SIMPLY:

Important Information You Need to Know for New Jersey Residents

By Linda C. Ashar, Attorney at Law

Mount Laurel Library
100 Walt Whitman Avenue
Mount Laurel, NJ 08054-9539
856-234-7319
www.mtlaurel.lib.nj.us

YOUR NEW JERSEY WILLS, TRUSTS, & ESTATES EXPLAINED SIMPLY: IMPORTANT INFORMATION YOU NEED TO KNOW FOR NEW JERSEY RESIDENTS

Copyright © 2012 Atlantic Publishing Group, Inc.
1210 SW 23rd Place • Ocala, Florida 34471 • Phone 800-814-1132 • Fax 352-622-1875
Website: www.atlantic-pub.com • E-mail: sales@atlantic-pub.com
SAN Number: 268-1250

No part of this publication may be reproduced, stored in a retrieval system, or transmitted in any form or by any means, electronic, mechanical, photocopying, recording, scanning, or otherwise, except as permitted under Section 107 or 108 of the 1976 United States Copyright Act, without the prior written permission of the Publisher. Requests to the Publisher for permission should be sent to Atlantic Publishing Group, Inc., 1210 SW 23rd Place, Ocala, Florida 34471.

Library of Congress Cataloging-in-Publication Data

Ashar, Linda C., 1947-
  Your New Jersey wills, trusts, & estates explained simply : important information you need to know for New Jersey residents / by Linda C. Ashar.
    p. cm.
  Includes bibliographical references and index.
  ISBN-13: 978-1-60138-420-1 (alk. paper)
  ISBN-10: 1-60138-420-3 (alk. paper)
  1. Estate planning--New Jersey--Popular works. I. Title.
  KFN1940.A974 2010
  332.024'01609749--dc22
                          2010027213

LIMIT OF LIABILITY/DISCLAIMER OF WARRANTY: The publisher and the author make no representations or warranties with respect to the accuracy or completeness of the contents of this work and specifically disclaim all warranties, including without limitation warranties of fitness for a particular purpose. No warranty may be created or extended by sales or promotional materials. The advice and strategies contained herein may not be suitable for every situation. This work is sold with the understanding that the publisher is not engaged in rendering legal, accounting, or other professional services. If professional assistance is required, the services of a competent professional should be sought. Neither the publisher nor the author shall be liable for damages arising herefrom. The fact that an organization or website is referred to in this work as a citation and/or a potential source of further information does not mean that the author or the publisher endorses the information the organization or website may provide or recommendations it may make. Further, readers should be aware that Internet websites listed in this work may have changed or disappeared between when this work was written and when it is read.

TRADEMARK DISCLAIMER: All trademarks, trade names, or logos mentioned or used are the property of their respective owners and are used only to directly describe the products being provided. Every effort has been made to properly capitalize, punctuate, identify, and attribute trademarks and trade names to their respective owners, including the use of ® and ™ wherever possible and practical. Atlantic Publishing Group, Inc. is not a partner, affiliate, or licensee with the holders of said trademarks.

PROJECT MANAGER: Melissa Peterson
PEER REVIEWER: Marilee Griffin
FRONT & BACK COVER DESIGN: Jackie Miller • millerjackiej@gmail.com

Printed on Recycled Paper

Printed in the United States

A few years back we lost our beloved pet dog Bear, who was not only our best and dearest friend but also the "Vice President of Sunshine" here at Atlantic Publishing. He did not receive a salary but worked tirelessly 24 hours a day to please his parents.

Bear was a rescue dog who turned around and showered myself, my wife, Sherri, his grandparents Jean, Bob, and Nancy, and every person and animal he met (well, maybe not rabbits) with friendship and love. He made a lot of people smile every day.

We wanted you to know a portion of the profits of this book will be donated in Bear's memory to local animal shelters, parks, conservation organizations, and other individuals and nonprofit organizations in need of assistance.

– Douglas & Sherri Brown

PS: We have since adopted two more rescue dogs: first Scout, and the following year, Ginger. They were both mixed golden retrievers who needed a home.

Want to help animals and the world? Here are a dozen easy suggestions you and your family can implement today:

- *Adopt and rescue a pet from a local shelter.*
- *Support local and no-kill animal shelters.*
- *Plant a tree to honor someone you love.*
- *Be a developer — put up some birdhouses.*
- *Buy live, potted Christmas trees and replant them.*
- *Make sure you spend time with your animals each day.*
- *Save natural resources by recycling and buying recycled products.*
- *Drink tap water, or filter your own water at home.*
- *Whenever possible, limit your use of or do not use pesticides.*
- *If you eat seafood, make sustainable choices.*
- *Support your local farmers markets.*
- *Get outside. Visit a park, volunteer, walk your dog, or ride your bike.*

Five years ago, Atlantic Publishing signed the Green Press Initiative. These guidelines promote environmentally friendly practices, such as using recycled stock and vegetable-based inks, avoiding waste, choosing energy-efficient resources, and promoting a no-pulping policy. We now use 100-percent recycled stock on all our books. The results: in one year, switching to post-consumer recycled stock saved 24 mature trees, 5,000 gallons of water, the equivalent of the total energy used for one home in a year, and the equivalent of the greenhouse gases from one car driven for a year.

DEDICATION

To my family. — Linda C. Ashar, attorney at law

AUTHOR BIOGRAPHY

Linda C. Ashar has practiced law for more than 25 years before the Ohio and federal bars. In addition to Atlantic Publishing Group Inc.'s estate planning series, she has also authored *101 Ways to Score Higher on Your LSAT: What You Need to Know About the Law School Admission Test Explained Simply*, *The Complete Power of Attorney Guide for Consumers and Small Businesses: Everything You Need to Know Explained Simply*, poetry, and several magazine and journal articles, including a collection on Suite101.com.

Ashar and her lawyer-husband Mike operate Thornapple Farms in Vermilion, Ohio, where they breed Morgan horses, Connemara ponies, and Irish Kerry Bog ponies, a critically endangered breed. Ashar serves on several nonprofit boards and is co-founder of the American Kerry Bog Pony Society. Reach her at ashar@hbr.net or lashar@wickenslaw.com.

TABLE OF CONTENTS

Chapter 8: Retirement Accounts 145

Chapter 9: Setting Priorities 161

Chapter 10: Choosing Who, What, How, When, and Why 175

Chapter 11: Planning Your Estate: Last Will and Testament in New Jersey 189

INTRODUCTION

Estate Planning: What is It?

Many estate-planning books suggest you begin the process by taking inventory of all the possessions you will leave behind. This does make a certain amount of sense, as disposing of these things according to your wishes is indeed a part of estate planning. The problem is that simply composing a list means you could end up with an extremely long list, including every single compact disc you own right now, not to mention the entire contents of your junk drawer. You might have some idea of what matters to you right now, but what about five months or 50 years from now?

Asking difficult questions and understanding your priorities are the two most important parts of estate planning. Whether you need a trust, additional life insurance, or a living will depends on what you want, not what a lawyer or an accountant tells you to do. Making such choices, though, can be difficult. Therefore, the first three chapters in this book are designed help you focus on the process of determining what you want.

Once you have a sense of the elements of estate planning that are important to you, then you have a reason to dig into the details about wills, beneficiaries, taxes, and all that other minutiae related to planning for whom you — not the courts or governments — want to benefit from your lifetime of hard work.

This book provides a common sense philosophy and approach to estate planning to give you a place to start. The first part of the book outlines a generalized overview of broadly applicable principles. As you will be reminded from time to time, several aspects of estate planning and provisions for your property at death are controlled by the laws of your state. *Chapter 11 focuses on the specific requirements for New Jersey residents.*

Throughout this book, you will see checklists, helpful tip boxes, and case studies by professionals or people in your similar situation to help you with the process of planning your estate. *Worksheets are provided in Appendix A.*

None of the information provided in this book is intended or should be interpreted to be legal advice. Each person's situation is unique and dependent on specific facts and circumstances. For legal advice specific to your situation, you must seek legal counsel from an attorney in your state who is specially trained or experienced in the field of estate planning and trusts.

Sandy Hook, Gateway National Recreation Area

CHAPTER 1
Getting Started

"Men in my family live well into their 70s, so I have plenty of time to do this."

"I created a will when my children were born. They are the only valuable 'possessions' I have, and they are already taken care of."

"This is only my third year in a full-time job. I have student loans to pay off and make no money. I do not have an estate to plan."

"We have been married for 12 years. If one of us dies before we get around to doing our estate planning, the spouse inherits everything — everyone knows that."

"Estate planning is for old people."

"I'll think about it tomorrow."

These typical reasons and evasions for not doing any type of estate planning are as varied and creative as the reasons concocted by children who did not do their homework. But unlike a teacher, who can excuse a missing paper, the state — the governmental body ultimately responsible for resolving all legal matters related to anything left behind by a person who has died — does not accept excuses from the next of kin, whether it be spouse, child, parents, or otherwise.

Statutes tell a judge how to distribute the ownership of real estate, pay credit card debts, satisfy mortgages, and also how to assign cash, Grandma's antique end table, and the boxes of personal papers stashed in the attic. To make matters more confusing, each state has at least a slightly different idea about how the process must to be handled, and Congress keeps changing the tax rules at the federal level.

According to estate-planning professionals, all the typical explanations for not doing estate planning are just excuses for avoiding two of the most taboo subjects in many cultures: money and death. With death comes feelings of fear, denial, and anger. With money comes the issues of self-worth, concern about the perceptions of others, and worries about the ability to support those who need help. These feelings and issues combine to create an emotional quagmire.

Pile on top of all that unfamiliar terminology, complicated tax laws, and a host of people who have their hands out for a chunk of your estate, and planning for what happens after your death is enough to cause anyone to exclaim, "The dog ate my estate plan."

Estate Planning Simplified

Like all complicated tasks, the best way to begin is to deal with individual pieces of information.

In simple terms, estate planning is the creation of a set of instructions about what should be done with your assets and personal belongings — including money, possessions, investments, collectibles, and anything else you own — before and after you die. It is more than just writing a will that distributes your best china and savings accounts; it is more than writing a to-do list of things you want done and bills that must be paid or finding a good asking price for your house or who you want to take care of your collie, Fluffy.

Anyone who has possessions, no matter how many or how few, needs to plan their estate. After you die, the mortgage payment still must be made, and your favorite charity is still going to need the new roof or donation you pledged — but you will not be there to write the checks. The bank and the charity will express sympathy to your family, but they will be looking for the benefit of their commitments. Your family will not know how you want these situations handled if you have not left instructions, nor will they be bound to follow your wishes if you have not sealed them into legal documents.

This thing called estate planning is just a continuation of what you do now — sharing yourself, your money, and your life experiences with the people and organizations that are important to you. Estate planning ensures the money and property you accumulated during your life can continue to serve your purposes after you can no longer direct matters yourself.

You can take action with your estate before you die, but some steps cannot be taken until after your death. Technical matters need to be considered, such as what taxes must be paid and how, in addition to distributing all your property. Before you can get to any of those details, you need to accept where you are in your life and that it will end at some point.

Everyone Dies: A Simple Statement with Complicated Implications

Some people embrace a philosophy that perceives death as a new adventure — the next step in living. Most people, though, do not see death, or even thinking about it, as fun or exciting. Thus, dying and all the trappings related to it rarely come up at the dinner table between "Pass the green beans," and "What's for dessert?" Given a choice between a conversation about death and clearing the dishes, people will fall over each other heading for the kitchen.

Like all things unfamiliar, the less death is discussed, the more taboo it becomes and the more uncomfortable people feel when it does come up. Avoiding the subject of death and what happens to those who are left behind only makes it a frightening topic. Like learning mathematical equations or the periodic table of elements in chemistry, practice and repetition can demystify the unknown and put it in a more calming perspective.

Numerous books cover death and dying. As these books have increased in number and popularity, some basic knowledge has crept into everyday language and consciousness. Dr. Elisabeth Kübler-Ross, who wrote *On Death and Dying*, mainstreamed the acceptance of grief as a reasonable, human emotion. She used grief — the sad, gut-wrenching feeling over losing someone loved or something cherished — to create a list of the emotional stages people experience when faced with a profound loss. These stages of grief have come to be embraced and recognized as normal and necessary in human experience.

The Five Stages of Grief

1. **Denial and isolation.** Disbelief that the loss has taken place and possible withdrawal from familiar routines and people.

2. **Anger.** Feeling furious at the person who inflicted the hurt or at the world for letting it happen; upset with self for allowing the loss to occur, even if nothing could have stopped it.

3. **Bargaining.** Attempting to negotiate with a higher power, saying, "If I do this, will you change the outcome, or bring about a miraculous solution?"

4. **Depression.** Feeling numb, lost, and unhappy. Anger and sadness may still be present.

5. **Acceptance.** All of the unsettled feelings calm down, maybe even fade, and the reality of the loss is finally acknowledged.

Even just imagining the loss of a loved one — as well as one's own death — can give rise to a semblance of these feelings. The advantage of facing these emotions is using the opportunity to face any self-doubt, fear, and anxiety that otherwise lurk either undetected or pushed beneath the events of day-to-day living.

Contemplating the inevitability of mortality need not be all doom and gloom, though. You can also use the process to think about the accomplishments, successes, and positive affects you have had and expect to have. The estate-planning process can enable you to develop a more realistic view of yourself, your values, and the fruits of your efforts. The act of planning empowers you to overcome any fears and worries about a seemingly dreary subject matter. You also can begin to see that even if you "cannot take it with you," the fruits of your labor have meaning and direction for you now.

Money Talk

Most adults do not want to include children in discussions of financial issues because they see it as a burden or scary subject for their children. However, without age-appropriate participation in conversations about family finances, children will never be guided in their learning about the role and impact of money. An exclusionary approach turns money into an off-limits topic. It also can make money appear to be the cause of problems, a bad thing, or even a big secret. Even worse, money can be viewed as "growing on trees."

By taking time to consider your past experiences with money, you can begin to understand the source of negative feelings or worries. You also can clarify the importance money has in your life. Decisions about the future will be difficult at best if you do not know what you want to accomplish — and disastrous if you make choices that are at odds with your true hopes and dreams or unrealistic for your circumstances.

One strong influence that can lead to misguided financial decisions is the proverbial "keeping up with the Joneses" mentality. Even if you do not think about painting your house to make it look as good as your neighbor's house that was just repainted, you most likely notice who has just repainted their house, who has a new car, and who is going on an exotic vacation. The amount of disposable income someone has can create a materialistic link between net worth and self-worth.

A benefit of estate planning is getting a realistic grasp on your present circumstances, as well as developing a concrete plan for the future.

I Do What with All This?

The point of giving serious thought to death and money is to sort through the mental and physical obstacles that cause you to put off planning your estate.

To avoid feeling overwhelmed, or perhaps to feel you are accomplishing something "hands on," such as collecting bank records, consider using a practical, logical method for collecting and organizing potentially emotional and volatile memories, experiences, thoughts, and preliminary, basic documents.

Lists

Consider topics that relate to you and your life situation; some suggestions are presented below. Create a list for each topic and organize the content into groups based on a common thread. Consider all possible angles for every topic, including past, present, and future. Be honest; nobody needs to see your lists but you. For example:

Money

Memories – childhood/family

- Mom and Dad arguing about the mortgage at the end of every month
- Getting a piggy bank from Grandma and money every birthday to "save for college"
- Handing the bank teller my savings book and a bag of pennies, and she smiled at me when she gave me a sucker
- Having my own Christmas Club bank account
- Having an allowance and giving part of it to the family church, synagogue, or favorite charity

Memories – adolescence

- Lemonade stand: math-class story problem turned Saturday afternoon project with friends, figuring out how to pay for ingredients and cups, how much to charge, and splitting the "profits" — I made my first dollar
- Being the only one who did not go on the class trip to Washington, D.C., because Dad was just laid off
- Working a summer job at a local grocery store

Adult experiences

- First car dying on the freeway and having no money to tow it
- Getting that first student loan payment book after graduation

- Photocopying first paycheck
- Overdrawing checking account
- Paying own rent and bills and having money left to send home

Dreams

- Owning a home
- Paying for in-home care for Mom and Dad (so they do not have to live with me)
- Having three children and sending them to college
- Spending a year abroad before I die
- Not having to worry about paying bills every month (is that even possible?)
- Having enough capital to start a business

Career versus job

Memories – childhood/family

- Work-ethic lectures from Grandpa while cleaning out the garage
- Grandma: "Put off work until tomorrow if you can play today"
- Uncle Jim who lived with us and never seemed to have a job
- Both Mom and Dad worked

Memories – adolescence

- Summer car wash for school fundraisers being hard work
- Career counselor at school insisting my test scores meant I would be an engineer
- Wanting to dance in the school musical
- Quitting marching band to play football

Adult experiences

- Trying to turn skateboarding hobby into a business
- Intense dislike of a micromanaging boss telling me what to do
- Feeling terrorized by bills
- Corporate downsizing

Dreams

- Having a job that supports me the rest of my life
- Not owning so much property that I need a storage locker to hold it
- A job that means I can support a family and spend time with them
- Retiring at 50

Other topics to focus on can be death, family, career, playtime/recreation, fears/worries, and anything else that evokes strong emotions as you consider other issues.

Journal

Choose a book with blank pages in which to record your estate-planning experience. Create sections for various stages in the process, leaving room for facts and figures, your feelings, and your thoughts. Leave space for doodling, notes, and pages of questions. Have pages for free association. For example, write "money" at the top of a page and write down what immediately comes to mind.

Stuff box

Find an old shoebox, or buy a special container for estate-planning material. Put in your lists, thoughts scribbled on the back of a napkin while drinking coffee, and your journal. This gives you a dedicated place for all the planning bits and pieces and documents when you need them, no matter what the form. If a movie ticket stub reminds you of the film documentaries you want to make someday, toss it in.

File folders

If you need more structure in your life, create a folder each time you address a topic, including getting ready to do your estate planning. Choose a family photo or a picture from a magazine that illustrates what matters most to you, and tape or staple one into each folder. If you get frustrated or annoyed, look at those pictures to remind yourself of why the work is necessary.

Use index cards to jot down thoughts, or digitally record your musings while you commute to and from work or sit outside by yourself on the porch, patio, yard, or beach — the method does not matter; it is doing the work that counts. Once you identify the factors that prevent you from planning for your death, you will be able to look more clearly at the present to help guide the future.

Here and Now

Beyond the tangle of complex emotions related to death and money, you need to figure out what is most important to you so that you can set some goals for what you want to happen after you die. How to go about doing that effectively depends on the individual and other people involved.

How one spouse views money can be dramatically different from the other spouse's viewpoint. The people and things you each value might differ as well. What is valuable can be difficult to define because of the way culture seems to place high importance on materialistic things. Creating a personal values list is one way to begin identifying what matters most to you.

For example, some people might write "Family matters most." However, things such as food, water, shelter, and medical care are necessary to survive. These things are important, but it does not mean they represent a "value" that you hold. To distinguish these points, consider the following definitions:

- **Need:** A requirement; a necessity
- **Want:** To desire deeply; to wish for
- **Value:** To hold in high regard; to appreciate and rate highly; a moral view

When you can distinguish between your needs, wants, and values, consider the role that values play in your daily life. Those things that you value tend to serve as the test or measuring stick for making decisions. When planning a summer vacation, do you feel it is more important to get away from daily stresses and relax in quiet with your immediate family, or is going on vacation without your parents and siblings never an option? Do you make sure you never miss extended-family events, such as weddings and graduations? You might value your extended family as highly as you do your immediate family, or your immediate family might be foremost in all decision-making. No one of these views is the "right" one. What is important is to understand which view is yours.

Stepping out of your everyday life to thoughtfully consider what makes up your everyday life is a way to gain perspective on what matters to you. Here are some matters to consider:

You

- Are you postponing something now, such as learning to paint, because you feel something else is more important, such as tutoring for your children?
- Are you a spiritual or religious person?

- Do you want your children to have everything you did not?
- Is your decision-making impulsive or thoughtful?
- Do you have time every day to do something you want to do? If not, why not?

Family

- How many children do you have or want to have? If you have children, is it possible you will have more someday, either by birth or adoption?
- What if infertility becomes an issue? Do you want to adopt or consider other options?
- Are you close to your parents? Siblings? Other relatives?
- What role does extended family play in your life?
- Are you particularly close to any relatives?
- Are you estranged from any relatives?
- Are any family members missing and their whereabouts unknown?
- Do you have children from a former marriage?
- Have you parented a child or children outside of legally recognized marriage?

Friends

- Are you close to people who are like family but not related by blood or marriage?
- Is "guys'/girls' night out/in" scheduled on a regular basis?
- Do you consult with one or more people about big changes you wish to make?
- Do you follow the advice of anyone in particular?
- Whom do you trust with your children when you are away?

Money

- What matters most to you — having enough money to pay the bills or having extra cash?
- Are you living paycheck to paycheck?
- How much money do you save from each paycheck?
- What retirement savings do you have, if any?
- How much debt do you have?

Community

- Is attending city council meetings a priority?
- Do you pick up trash when you are out walking the dog?
- When do you check a community calendar — when you are looking for a garage sale or trying to find something to do on a weeknight?
- Do you belong to a specific religious tradition to which you give your time and talents?
- When was the last time you chatted with a neighbor?
- Are you a member of any nonprofit boards?
- Do you volunteer for a school or charity?

The practical decisions to be made about your estate, such as who will get what, can gradually become clear as you sort out what is a feeling, what is important, and who is in your life. Instead of being caught up in whether the size of your estate will confirm your father's prediction that you would always be a screw-up, you can see how important he is to your family and that you want to do whatever you can to help care for him — before and after you die.

Separating facts from feelings will make it possible to see the opportunities and benefits that planning has to offer.

• *Did You Know?* •

At some point, most people have taken a personality assessment test. In high school, they were designed to direct clueless teenagers toward a specific career path. Magazines claim they can identify your ideal mate based on a ten-question survey that identifies your personality based on the Myers-Briggs typology.

When assessments for the workplace gained popularity in the 1980s, your human resources department might have rolled out a company-wide assessment program to help managers better understand and communicate with employees on a daily basis or to help them work through disputes. Lumped into one of four groups associated with a flavor of ice cream — "Are you a vanilla, too? Bo is a chocolate and Pat is a strawberry. No wonder my department is so messed up!" — the results seemed more gimmicky than informative and helpful.

Over time, research and development have refined and specialized these assessments to the point where the results provide surprisingly accurate, functional information about individual values and interests. If you are struggling with shifting priorities or feeling confused about how to deal with changes in your life, this is one tool that can offer some insight and direction.

Put This to Use

If you have trouble creating a values-list worksheet or putting into words what you feel is most important in your life, taking an assessment might help.

Choosing an assessment tool can be difficult when you do not know where to look. The most reputable companies work with certified professionals — social workers, psychologists, coaches — whom they train to select the best assessment to provide the kind of information you need. The specialist will then talk through the results with you, asking questions and offering suggestions about how to use the results.

TTI Success Insights® is an assessment company that offers an assessment called Personal Interests, Attitudes and Values ™. These assessments are not free, but the information they provide can be valuable.

What This Work Can Do

Change is difficult for most people on a good day, but under the influence of grief, it can be impossible to accomplish the most mundane tasks of cooking meals and taking out the garbage. At some point in the future, your family and close friends will be in that same position when dealing with your death.

Maybe your family will prefer to wear red, yellow, and bright orange to the memorial service. They might even make a family trip out of scattering your ashes on the Atlantic Ocean. Regardless of how your family will choose to cope with your death, there are steps you can take to allow them the freedom to do what they need to.

You can plan and pay for your funeral ahead of time. Perhaps you will be able to arrange to polish off the mortgage, make sure your mother's assisted-living bills are paid so she can spend her retirement money on cruises, add a new wing to the church, or set up a foundation to make sure your community council has an endowment for improved living conditions.

Estate planning can also help now. By clarifying your priorities now, you can plan and save in ways that will allow you to realize your goals during your lifetime for your own pleasure and satisfaction, as well as after you die. Estate planning can:

- Integrate and organize all your goals — personal, professional, financial, and estate
- Preserve your assets for use now and in the future

- Provide for your family and any chosen charities
- Ensure the efficient distribution of your estate the way you want it distributed
- Save money for your estate's obligations — taxes, legal fees, and court costs, for example

What Exactly is Involved

Each estate plan is different. Just as no people are identical, there are no one-size-fits-all estate plans. They have similar components, and numerous books have been written about every possible aspect of estate planning.

Also, depending on where you live, laws come into play to affect what you can do with your property and when you can do this. This book is geared toward New Jersey residents.

The chapters that follow cover the basic process and some of the more detailed information about the elements of an estate plan to assist you in creating your own. This, like any other book or template, ought to be a resource for gathering information and generating ideas. To adopt a canned plan that is sold as "cheap and easy" is to get what you pay for — a bad fit and not the outcome you hope to achieve.

The goal of this book is to help you do your homework and familiarize you with terminology to ask questions of and have discussions with your estate-planning professionals. If you want to do the job right, find people you can trust with your hopes and dreams.

This book is not is a substitute for legal advice. It provides general information for guidance to assist in planning how you want to arrange your personal estate for yourself and posterity. Laws change, and how they are applied depends on a person's individual circumstances and place of residence. Do not rely on any statement in this book as specific legal advice.

CASE STUDY: HIRING AN ESTATE-PLANNING COACH

Patricia Beaugard, Executive Coach & Trainer
pat@patbeaugard.com
www.patbeaugard.com

Patricia Beaugard has extensive experience in the field of personal and professional coaching, in addition to being a trained ITT assessment specialist. She shares some of her thoughts on how a coach can be an important part of your estate-planning team.

Facing death

Many people have a difficult time facing the idea of their own death, so they avoid things that will remind them of it, like estate planning. Shifting the focus onto the people who are left behind, their survivors, is a way to focus on helping them. Ask, "What can I do to help my loved ones get through this difficult time in their lives?"

It can be helpful to look at what is bothering you: What is holding you back? What are your fears? All of these things indicate some underlying concerns; they might be related to dying, to money, or maybe to your family members. How much you will delve into these topics is based on individual preferences.

Making notes about your feelings and the thoughts that come up when you think about estate planning can be part of the process of identifying what you have, to whom it will be given, and how your possessions will be distributed. And it needs to be a process: Make some notes, then set them aside for a few days or weeks. Go back to them after you have had time to think about these things before you ask yourself, "Is this what I really want? Am I clear on this?"

Money, stuff, and meaning

Money represents something of value because of what it can be used for. Actually, it is a form of energy. Many people work hard for their money and are attached to it — they might struggle with the idea of "giving it away" to others because it represents their accomplishments and work. For those who can see money as energy, it can flow to others because they can always get more.

People make decisions based on their emotions and their feelings. Sometimes they are not even aware of the feelings they have, so it can be helpful for another person to help them sort out those feelings. After you share your thoughts and feelings about a specific issue — like not wanting to distribute your estate — another person can share his or her impressions of your concerns. In that way, talking can help you explore how you feel and observe the influence those feelings have on your decision, or lack thereof.

Some people get quite passionate. That is when making time and space to step away and thoughtfully consider feelings and decisions is helpful; you can better determine whether that passion is a serious priority or a passing impulse brought on by the estate-planning process. Consider:

- Where did this passion come from?
- Has this passion been a lasting influence?
- How have you lived this passion in your life?

I have a friend in Seattle who has never had children, but she has always had dogs, and all of them are rescued animals. For her vacation, she went to spend time with an organization in Utah that rescues all kinds of animals. She spent a week volunteering there, and she supports the organization financially. This is truly a value of hers because she supports it in word and deed.

Motivators and values

By looking more deeply at what matters to you — your values — you will find what drives (or motivates) you to choose the profession you are in, where you live, or the kind of volunteer work you do for which organizations.

Another way to approach this process is considering who and what is important in your life: extended family, nonblood "relatives," faith or spirituality, hobbies, the items you collect, or the traveling you do.

For people who have difficulty talking about or identifying these details, written assessments can help them determine their values in a concrete way. Do you care about making a difference in society? Not everyone does, but some people are quite driven by that. Are you focused on making sure your family has financial resources available to them, or do you value independence and want to foster that in your family? Maybe you see leaving your estate to your family as "spoiling" them.

What matters to you now might change in a few years — just look at the people or things you could never do without several years ago and compare that to your life now. As a result, revisiting your motivators and values on a regular basis is important, and a coach can do more than remind you to take that second, third, and fourth look — he or she can ask you the questions you might forget to ask yourself so that your review is thorough.

Finding a coach

A life coach helps you look at and consider these complicated, difficult topics in a constructive manner. When choosing a coach, you want to decide what criteria are important to you. Do you want to work with a coach whom others have recommended? Do you want your coach to be certified? Do you want someone who has graduated from a coach-training program? What kind of background or experience is important in your eyes?

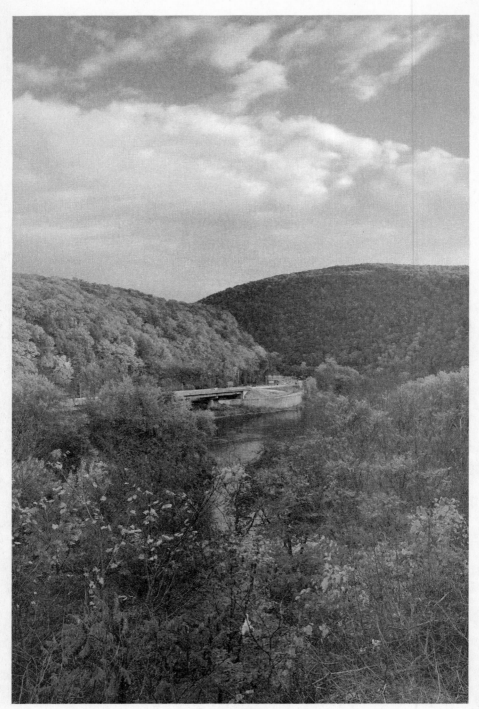

Delaware Water Gap

CHAPTER 2

Estate-Planning Basics

According to a recent survey conducted by Harris Interactive:

- 55 percent of adult Americans do not have a will.

- 68 percent of adult African-Americans do not have a will.

- 74 percent of adult Hispanic-Americans do not have a will.

- 59 percent of adults do not have a living will.

- 62 percent of adults do not have a power of attorney for health care purposes.

- 10 percent of adults who have not prepared any part of an estate plan say it is because they do not wish to think about dying or becoming incapacitated.

- 9 percent of adults say they do not have an estate plan because they do not know who to talk to about creating one.

- 24 percent of adults say they have not created an estate plan because they lack the sufficient assets to require one.

The primary fact that these numbers reveal is that most people do not plan for their deaths or what happens to their money and possessions after they are no longer around to call the shots. The reasons are likely among those discussed in the previous chapter and more. Certainly, many people view estate planning either as complicated, frightening, or only for the very rich.

However, estate planning is neither mysterious nor incomprehensible. It certainly is not a privilege reserved for the wealthy. Everyone can have a will. Everyone can plan for the future.

Even though estate planning does encompass a broad array of potentially complicated issues, such as federal tax law and "boilerplate" legal language required by courts, you do not need to become an expert in all these areas to have a valid will and an estate plan. The most important thing to recall is the simple foundation on which all of this rests: When you die, your property stays here and so do the people you love. You have a right to determine what happens with these things.

Of course, you can be buried with your platinum credit card or favorite jewelry, and you might even be able to arrange to be buried in your car, but the taxes and balances due on debts or liabilities must be paid and the rest of your property must go somewhere. Your spouse and children, if you have them, might have legal claims, and all of these considerations are part of your estate.

Suppose you want your son to have your house, and you give him the keys. Sounds like "possession," right? Everyone one has heard the old saying, "possession is 9/10 of the law," so will this work? Unfortunately, your son cannot claim to own the family house simply by saying, "She gave me the keys before she died and said it is mine." If you do not transfer the title to his name by executing the necessary legal documents with the required legal formalities, then legally, the house is still yours. If you have not named him as beneficiary in your will, and you have other heirs besides your son or you have creditors who claim the house for payment, then your son is not likely to get it.

Without doing the necessary legal paperwork, your belongings are still your belongings — your debts and your assets — and if you die without a will, the state will dispose of all of them according to law because you are no longer around to do it yourself.

Beyond the material items are the unexpected and potentially more complicated issues leading up to your death. A heart attack or car accident could result in brain death, a coma. Who makes the decision about your medical care and the use of extraordinary means to extend your life?

The best way to ensure that your wishes will be carried out is to make them known and in such a way that there is no doubt about what they are. But first, you must learn the facts about what you can and cannot do, as well as methods to ensure that your wishes will be followed.

Debunking Myths

People will do, say, and believe just about anything to avoid doing things they do not want to do; estate planning is no exception. Perhaps this is how so many myths about death and taxes came into being.

- **Myth: The estate tax — the "death tax" — was repealed, so there are no taxes to avoid anymore.** The federal estate tax law was repealed for one year at the beginning of 2010, according to the Economic Growth and Tax Relief Reconciliation Act, passed into law in 2001. If you happened to have died during 2010, then you would not have had to pay federal estate taxes, but your estate would still have been subject to any estate taxes that might have been imposed by New Jersey. The federal estate tax returns in 2011 operate according to the same law, unless Congress makes changes, which could occur by the time or after this book has gone to print. *Chapter 4 has more information about taxes.*

- **Myth: All I need is a will — it will take care of all my assets.**
  Debts do not go away; even if a will sets aside money to pay those debts, it might not be sufficient. In that case, the assets in your estate, such as your grandchild's college fund, will be tapped to pay creditors. Additionally, a will only addresses property that is in your name — meaning your name is the only one listed on the title as the owner. Property that is owned jointly with survivorship rights or pay-on-death (POD) beneficiaries — such as real estate, retirement accounts, or life insurance policies — will pass to the surviving owner or go to a beneficiary. *Chapter 5 goes into more detail about wills in general and Chapter 11 speaks specifically to New Jersey wills.*

- **Myth: Trusts are for wealthy people.** A trust can be created by anyone who has an asset or assets (otherwise known collectively as "the res") to make the subject of the trust. A trust can eliminate or dramatically reduce the amount of estate taxes that will be paid by your survivors and/or your estate if it is set up properly during your lifetime. Choosing the right type of trust to suit your needs and applying careful adherence to legal language will make a trust a viable option for anyone. *Chapter 6 further addresses trusts.*

- **Myth: Life insurance is not subject to estate tax, so I do not need to do any other planning.** Life insurance proceeds frequently are not subject to income tax if they are paid to someone else, like a spouse, parents, or a charitable institution. However, if you own a life insurance policy and you have not named a beneficiary, then the proceeds of that policy become part of your taxable estate and will be subject to state and federal estate tax. Any person who receives the insurance proceeds will likely receive those proceeds without incurring any income tax liability unless it is in a state that makes it subject to inheritance tax. Also, a beneficiary of insurance proceeds who has paid the premiums might be taxed on the proceeds minus the amount of the premiums paid. *Chapter 7 elaborates more on insurance.*

- **Myth: If I do not name a beneficiary for my 401(k), my spouse still gets the money.** Assets that do not have a named beneficiary in a will or some other legal document will end up in probate court as part of your estate. This might benefit your spouse — or not. If you want your spouse or some other person to receive the unused portion of any retirement savings accounts, then he or she must be named as a beneficiary. Naming a second, or backup, beneficiary will also keep the account out of probate if the primary beneficiary is already deceased or declines the gift for some reason. *Including your retirement accounts into your estate plan is covered in Chapter 8.*

- **Myth: If I die without a will, my spouse gets everything.** In some states this might be true, but in most states it is not if there are also living children (or their descendants) of both the deceased and the surviving spouse and sometimes other heirs. The laws of the state in which you live will determine who gets what, and creditors tend to be paid first. If you own property in two or more states — maybe a condo in Florida, a house in New Jersey, and a cottage in Michigan, for example — the courts of each state might become involved in the distribution of your assets because they each have primary jurisdiction over the land in their state. *Probate court and its role with your estate are explained in Chapter 11.* It is never a good idea to make "simple" assumptions about how probate matters work, especially without a will directing the deceased's wishes.

Misinformation and half-truths abound, especially with the continuous changes in estate tax laws at state and federal levels. Anything you think you already know about estate planning can become obsolete without you ever being aware of it. Over time, most people buy and sell possessions such as houses, stock portfolios, antiques, and vehicles, and those changes are called a changeling. Whether your estate is growing or diminishing, you need to understand what you have, how and when it changes, and how you want it to be handled after your death.

Your Estate

Yes, you have one, and defining it will most likely be the most straightforward part of this process. Your estate is made up of everything you own, or your entire worth in a numerical sense. The formula for figuring out your net worth — a person's true financial value — is theoretically simple:

$$\textbf{Assets} - \textbf{Liabilities} = \textbf{Net worth}$$

Asset: Anything a person owns or is owed; this can be money, real estate, investments, or any other tangible property.

Liability: A debt or an obligation to pay money to another person or institution; also called a negative balance.

Following are some examples of common assets and liabilities:

Assets

- Annuities
- Cars
- Cash
- Certificates of deposit
- Insurance
- Investments

- Collectibles (e.g., coin collections, stamp collections)
- Personal property (e.g., jewelry or household items)
- Real estate
- Rental income
- Retirement funds
- Savings/checking accounts
- Stock certificates
- Structured settlements (e.g., lottery winnings or lawsuit settlements)

Liabilities

Bills/debts:

- Alimony
- Automobile payments
- Child support
- Credit card balances
- Future debt (e.g., a child's college tuition or care of parents)
- Student loans
- Insurance premiums
- Mortgages (first- and second-home equities)
- Business indemnifications
- Cosigner obligations (as for a family member or friend)
- Personal loans
- Taxes

Because it is important to keep your list of assets up-to-date, you might consider using a digital camera to make a visual inventory of your assets so that you can create an archive of these items. When documenting a dollar value for each item, such as the appraisal of a necklace, you can scan that appraisal and make it part of the electronic archive. You also can collect and scan any other documents, such as stock certificates, purchase invoices, or a house deed.

These documents will be essential when meeting with estate-planning advisors, so collecting them in a secure, fireproof safe as you build your inventory will save time later.

People

You never know how many friends you have until you win the lottery; the same can be true about your death. Some people never know how many creditors, lost family, and illegitimate children they supposedly had until their will is made part of the public record. After your death is legally certified, your will must be filed with the court, where it becomes public record. Anyone who wants to make a claim against your estate can, which is when the real work begins for those who helped you with your planning.

To make sure your wishes will be understood and carried out, you need to make sure that the people who are connected with your estate planning do as you chose, not what is most convenient for them.

Paid professional planners and those who carry out your wishes, such as executors, secondary executors, or legal guardians — and others, such as the court, creditors, and beneficiaries — will have a say in what happens after you are gone. Some people are outside your control, such as the court judge and unforeseen claimants, but you can choose those who will serve as the representatives who manage your estate.

Estate-planning professionals

Yes, there are people who actually enjoy estate-planning work. What might seem like torture to you is a challenging, rewarding career for someone who likes helping people sort out and plan for the future. The fees they charge can be an hourly rate, a per-document fee, or an ongoing estate-management fee. Be sure you understand what the charges are and how they are paid — and, if there is a contract, read the fine print.

Lawyer

Also called attorneys, lawyers can specialize in specific aspects of estate planning, such as wills, trusts, or probate procedure, or they might have a broader focus, such as estate planning or tax law. Depending on the size of your estate, you might need to consult with more than one lawyer to make sure all the legal issues related to your estate are properly prepared for. Some law firms have multiple members who can do all your work in-house under the direction of your lead lawyer. Or you might feel more comfortable having different firms work on different parts of your estate plan. No matter how you approach this process, you need to be forthcoming about all your personal goals and estate-planning wishes with everyone involved so that the work on the various areas support, not undermine or contradict, each other.

Certified public accountant (CPA)

Accountants can specialize in various aspects of financial estate matters such as trusts, annuities, and estate tax law, but they also serve as estate-planning specialists who can help you consider all financial decisions. An accountant must be current on tax law and other legal requirements related to accounting for money. Like a law firm, an accounting firm can have several people on staff who specialize in different areas. But the same caution applies: Be comfortable with your CPA, because he or she has to be trusted with all the same personal information if he or she is going to work well with others on your team.

Financial planner

There are all types of financial planners out there with initials after their names, such as Certified Financial Planner® (CFP®), Chartered Financial Analyst (CFA), and some without initials. However, all of them analyze a person's overall financial situation and develop a comprehensive plan in conjunction with the individual, designed to meet his or her financial goals and objectives. Certified planners have followed a specific course of education or training classes, and some go on to develop expertise in specific areas, such as estate or retirement planning. Financial planners can help you prepare your estate to achieve a target goal for a certain age or projected time-of-death value that you want to leave behind. Be wary of anyone who is self-taught or works on 100 percent commission; the advice you get might not necessarily be based on the most current information or in your best interest. Commissioned salespeople have an interest in selling specific products to earn their livelihoods, which will not necessarily coincide with your needs or your pocketbook.

Insurance agent

Gone are the days when an insurance salesperson appeared at your door and offered to spend hours chatting with you about your insurance needs — home, auto, and life being the basics. Today, many representatives go through human resource departments to communicate long-term and short-term disability coverage for company employees, which might be partially paid for by the employer. Medical and dental insurance — not to mention pet insurance, long-term care insurance, and other less common insurance plans — are now sold over the phone or on the Internet. An actual insurance agent can help you with your estate plan by assessing the type and amount of insurance you need and can afford. A real agent, rather than a call-center staffer, is the better person to speak to your insurance needs, but if you cannot find one, your other estate-planning professionals might be able to help.

Coaches

Financial, professional, and personal coaches can help you identify and manage monetary, career, and personal goals. At a time when mixed messages about being loyal to your employer and diversifying your stock portfolio make you wonder what you should do about the stock options your company offers, a coach can help you sort out the implications of selling or keeping those options and the potential impact on your career and estate plan. Their goal is to see you succeed, not make sure a corporation thrives or your beneficiaries get a chunk of change. A coach is an objective third party who, at the same time, is hired to focus primarily on what is best for you. Again, considering training and being able to communicate comfortably with the coach are critical to finding someone who will be a good fit for your needs. There are certification courses for various forms of coaching, but there are no national standards, and formal training is not required to present oneself as a coach. This means you must ask some specific questions about the person's experience, training, and references.

Spiritual advisor

The altruistic efforts of many people are based on their chosen faith traditions or their own moral compasses. Some types of difficult decisions about personal matters are not always accounting or purely legal issues. For example, you might be trying to decide whether your drug-addicted brother will be helped or hurt by a large inheritance as part of your estate planning. Choosing charitable institutions to benefit from your life's work might be another consideration. Changes in your life, such as divorce or the unexpected death of a loved one, might necessitate changes in your will at a time when the family member you would normally discuss these issues with is grieving. A minister, priest, rabbi, or other faith consultant can offer guidance, support, and information related to your belief system that might be helpful in these situations. Someone to talk to about personal matters related to family decisions especially speaks to the values and priorities you have identified early in the estate-planning process.

Whether you need any or all of these people in their various roles to participate in your estate plan is up to you and the types of issues that arise in process. Though some do not charge anything, others might have flat rates or hourly charges. The money you invest, much like the time you invest, is valuable, so be sure you weigh the short-term costs against the long-term gains.

If you choose to use more than one person to assist with your planning, consider choosing one person to serve as the primary contact through which all information will flow. If you choose a lawyer to serve as your point person, which is usually the best choice, he or she would work with the other professionals on your team to collect and ask for clarification about their part of your estate management. Then, he or she would meet with you and, at one time, go through all the information. A time-saving efficiency for you, this will cost a little extra because you need to pay your lawyer to do this coordination, but in the long run, you will have a reliable, well-informed person who can serve in your stead when you are gone and who understands the complete picture of your estate and your intentions.

☑ Choosing an Estate Planner

Estate-Planner Qualities and Characteristics

Qualifications for estate-planning professionals will vary based on their professional focus and expertise. Individual training is important, but all of them should have some fundamental skills. Scrutinize prospective estate-planning team members before and after you meet them — they will be privy to your most personal and private information.

Before: Do some homework before you meet with a planner.

☐ Is your estate planner ethical? Check with the Better Business Bureau and any related professional organizations, such as the American Bar Association for lawyers, to find out whether any complaints have been filed or reprimand proceedings have taken place.

☐ How well does your planner interact with clients? Get references for current clients to inquire about the positives and negatives of working with this person. Some questions to ask his or her current clients might be:

- o Is this person prepared for meetings, and does he or she follow-through on tasks that need to be done afterward?

- o How well does this person collaborate with other estate-planning professionals?

- o Do you spend much time in the waiting area before an appointment?

o   Have you ever had mistakes occur with your invoices?

o   Have your meetings ever been canceled on short notice?

☐   What professional associations is your planner a part of? If this person is the member of an organization, call and inquire about his or her involvement and whether the organization can make any referrals.

☐   What services does your planner offer? Find out the range of services this person offers, or whether he or she works in collaboration with others inside or outside his or her company.

☐   Is your planner considerate? Being willing to listen to your concerns and needs is essential; review his or her website or any promotional materials for signs of this trait.

After: When you meet with an estate-planning professional for the first time, pay attention to the level of comfort or discomfort you feel, and evaluate that meeting soon afterward. These are a few questions to consider:

☐   Did he or she ask you relevant questions?

☐   Which did he or she do more, talk or listen?

☐   Did he or she tell you what you should do, or present you with options to consider?

☐   Did he or she disclose any commissions or other considerations he or she receives from the institutions offering the products he or she represents? For example, he or she presents three different kinds of life insurance; for one of those, he or she will receive a commission if you sign on the dotted line.

☐   Did he or she explain things in a way that you could understand?

☐   Was he or she willing to go back over details until you were clear about confusing points?

☐   Were you given fees and hourly rates in writing?

☐   Are you expected to sign a contract?

☐   Were you given a timeline or some other expectation about how long this process might take?

☐   Did you feel you were being helped, or seen as nothing more than a revenue stream?

CASE STUDY: WHAT IT TAKES TO BE A FINANCIAL ADVISOR

U.S. Department of Labor
Bureau of Labor Statistics
www.dol.gov

Estate planning is a specialty within the field of financial planning, and the U.S. Department of Labor, via the Bureau of Labor Statistics, predicts this will be a growth industry for many years to come.

Beyond that, the bureau also provides job descriptions and other information about various industries, including financial advisors and planners. This material provides a description of the kind of work a planner might do in a day and the characteristics of a person who is successful in this kind of position. You might not be looking to make a career change, but this can serve as excellent background material when you begin looking for an estate planner to help you develop your plan.

Financial analysts and personal financial advisors

Significant points:

- Good interpersonal skills and an aptitude for working with numbers are among the most important qualifications for financial analysts and personal financial advisors.
- Keen competition is anticipated for these highly paid positions, despite rapid job growth; those who have earned a professional designation or an MBA are expected to have the best opportunities.
- Almost one-third of personal financial advisors are self-employed.

Nature of the work

Financial analysts and personal financial advisors provide analysis and guidance to businesses and individuals in making investment decisions. Both types of specialists gather financial information, analyze it, and make recommendations. However, their job duties differ because of the type of investment information they provide and their relationships with investors.

Personal financial advisors assess the financial needs of individuals. Advisors use their knowledge of investments, tax laws, and insurance to recommend financial options to individuals. They help them identify and plan to meet short- and long-term goals. Planners help clients with retirement and estate planning, funding the college education of children, and general investment choices. Many also provide tax advice or sell life insurance. Although most planners offer advice on a wide range of topics, some specialize in areas such as retirement and estate planning or risk management.

Personal financial advisors tend to work with many clients, and they often must find their own customers. Many personal financial advisors spend a great deal of their time making sales calls and marketing their services. Many advisors also meet potential clients by giving seminars or lectures, or through business and social contacts. Finding clients and building a customer base is one of the most important aspects of becoming successful as a financial advisor.

Financial advisors begin work with a client by setting up a consultation. This is often an in-person meeting in which the advisor obtains as much information as possible about the client's finances and goals. The advisor then develops a comprehensive financial plan that identifies problem areas, makes recommendations for improvement, and selects appropriate investments compatible with the client's goals, attitude toward risk, and expectation or need for a return on the investment. Sometimes this plan is written, but more often it is in the form of verbal advice. Advisors sometimes meet with accountants or legal professionals for help.

Financial advisors tend to meet with established clients at least once a year to update them on potential investments and to adjust their financial plan to any life changes — such as marriage, disability, or retirement. Financial advisors also answer clients' questions regarding changes in benefit plans or the consequences of a change in their jobs or careers. Financial planners must educate their clients about risks and various possible scenarios so that the clients do not harbor unrealistic expectations.

Most personal financial advisors buy and sell financial products, such as securities and life insurance. Fees and commissions from the purchase and sale of securities and life insurance plans are one of the major sources of income for most personal financial advisors.

Education and training

A bachelor's or graduate degree is required for financial analysts and is strongly preferred for personal financial advisors.

Employers usually do not require a specific field of study for personal financial advisors, but a bachelor's degree in accounting, finance, economics, business, mathematics, or law provides good preparation for the occupation. Courses in investments, taxes, estate planning, and risk management are also helpful. Programs in financial planning are becoming more widely available in colleges and universities.

Licensure

Almost all personal financial advisors need the Series 7 and Series 63 or 66 licenses. These licenses give their holders the right to act as a registered representative of a securities firm and to give financial advice. Because the Series 7 license requires sponsorship, self-employed personal financial advisors must maintain a relationship with a large securities firm. This relationship allows them to act as representatives of that firm in the buying and selling of securities.

If personal financial advisors choose to sell insurance, they need additional licenses issued by state licensing boards.

Other qualifications

Strong math, analytical, and problem-solving skills are essential qualifications for financial analysts. Good communication skills also are necessary, because these workers must present complex financial concepts and strategies. Self-confidence, maturity, and the ability to work independently are important, as well. Financial analysts must be detail-oriented, motivated to seek out obscure information, and familiar with the workings of the economy, tax laws, and money markets. Financial analysts should also be comfortable with computers because computers often ease complex financial tasks. Although much of the software financial analysts use is proprietary, they must be comfortable working with spreadsheets and statistical packages.

Personal financial advisors need many of the same skills, but they must emphasize customer service. They need strong sales skills, including the ability to make customers feel comfortable. It is important that they can present financial concepts to clients in easy-to-understand language. Personal financial advisors must also be able to interact casually with people from many different backgrounds. Some advisors have experience in a related position, such as accountant, auditor, insurance sales agent, or broker.

Who Will Carry Out Your Wishes in Your Place?

At the heart of estate planning is the recognition that at some point, you will die, and before then, you might become incompetent. Should either event happen, someone else has to take responsibility for your estate. This responsibility will involve both people and property.

Determining who will serve as the legal guardian of minor children is a huge decision and a tremendous responsibility for the person who agrees to be responsible for the health and well-being of your children. A guardian of a minor — any adult legally appointed to be responsible for the needs of children until they reach legal age — is not the same as a guardian for an adult. The guardian of an adult is any adult who can be legally appointed to manage the affairs of an incompetent or infirm adult of any age. A mentally challenged 32-year-old brother can need a guardian as much as a parent in the early stages of Alzheimer's disease.

Equally important is the executor of your estate. An executor, also called a personal representative, is the individual who handles the property you leave behind. If you die without a will, the court appoints an administrator — frequently a spouse or adult child. This person's fiduciary obligation is to make sure your assets and liabilities are disposed of in a legal, efficient, and thoughtful manner. The money necessary to support your children, a disabled sibling, or your aging parents will be in the hands of your executor.

Legal guardians

Whether for a child or an adult, appointing the guardianship of another person is legal action: The court appoints a guardian based on the wishes of the person making the request. A child's godparents do not automatically become guardians upon your death; you have to put guardianship in writing in a will. If you are the legal guardian of your elderly mother, you need to make provisions for her care in your will in the event that you might die before she does.

The guardian for a minor will be responsible for items such as food, clothing, and shelter. However, he or she also will be responsible for managing assets in the child's name and providing for things such as education and health care. The same can be true for the guardian of an adult, who might also be responsible for paying bills and making sure the adult's home is cleaned on a regular basis.

Choosing any guardian is difficult because of the responsibilities involved. The most obvious concern is selecting someone who will care for your family the way you would, but more important is whether the person will follow through on the commitment. A person in her 20s in the midst of building a career might say she is willing to set aside her career to care for her sister's young children, but after three years will she still be willing to stay at home with the children, even though money is not an issue?

Consider some of the following:

- **Age:** Young and old are as much about experience as birth date. Do you want the person taking care of your children to be your same age?

- **Lifestyle:** Your sister is nonreligious, but you want your children to attend a Catholic church. Will she take them to church every Sunday?

- **Child-rearing/caring-for-adult skills:** Patience is essential, as is the savvy to know where to find and seek help as needed. Is the person you are considering good with children?

- **Marital status:** Your divorced brother is fabulous with your boys, but would two parents be better for your children? Would your sister and her husband be better?

- **Compatibility:** If your children hate your sister's husband, this is not going to be a good long-term fit. How do your children act around the person you are considering?

- **Money skills:** Your aunt is a penny pincher, but your uncle is a spendthrift. Will the money set aside for your brother's group-home bills last under their watch?

You also need to consider your expectations for your children and how much of those you want to impose on the people who will become their new parents. After you decide upon the priorities for your children, make a list of several people and ask each of them whether they would be willing to serve as guardians under the conditions that you lay out. It is a bad idea to name someone as guardian without his or her knowledge. If that person refuses, the court will then decide what is in the best interest of the minors or others in need of care. The people the court chooses might not be to your liking.

A secondary or "backup" guardian will address the gap left by people who might be unable to serve in that capacity.

New Jersey has specific guardianship laws enacted in 2006. Inherent in New Jersey's approach to guardianship is a zealous interest in a person's right to dignity and self-determination.

New Jersey also allows parents or existing guardians to nominate what is called a "standby guardian," a person to act in their stead upon the occurrence of a triggering event. N.J. Ann. Stat. § 3B:12-72 provides for a petition to the court for appointment of the standby guardian. The petition must identify:

- The event(s) whose occurrence will cause the appointment of the standby guardian to become active and effective

- The significant risk that the present parent or lawful custodian of the minor or custodial person will die, become incapacitated, or become debilitated due to a progressive chronic disease, condition, or illness

- The name, address, contact information, and qualifications of the proposed standby guardian to take on the guardianship responsibility

Children age 14 or older must be notified within 30 days of the filing of the standby appointment petition, and the court will be the final determiner of the appointment. Therefore, stating the reasons and qualifications for the appointment of the standby guardian are an important feature of the petition. Two witnesses are required to the designator of guardian's signature.

• *Did You Know?* •

A property guardian or property manager is a legal adult who takes responsibility for the oversight of property inherited by a minor/child. Children under the age of 18 can inherit property, but they are only allowed to legally own that property with adult supervision; an adult must have the responsibility of managing it. Just because a 17-year-old can inherit a car does not mean he or she is "in charge."

The responsibility of becoming the legal guardians of a minor child or children might be enough for the people you select to provide for their upbringing. If the burden of managing their property on top of that is too much, another person can be appointed for that role.

Put This to Use

> Harry and Sally set up an education trust for their three minor children — Huey, Dewy, and Louis — in addition to putting the house and all other assets in their names. They are enrolled in private schools and will continue to live in their home; Aunt Blanche is moving in with them.
>
> Blanche has a good heart but is bad with money — so bad that she forgets to make her own house payment. Putting her in charge of making sure the tuition is paid from the proper accounts and the property taxes are paid on time is a disaster waiting to happen. So, Harry and Sally named their long-time banker and trust officer, Bill Smith, as the property manager. He also knows Blanche, so she can easily call him to ask for help if any additional school fees need to be paid. This frees her to focus on the boys instead of on the finances.
>
> An added bonus is that Bill, as a trust officer for a bank, is not likely to get away with embezzling money from the trusts. Bill cannot be paid a fee, which means more money for the trust.

☑ Choosing a Guardian

You, your children, a sibling, or a parent might one day need another person to make decisions that you — or they — would normally make. Asking someone else to take on your responsibilities in addition to their own is a significant request that carries legal, ethical, and moral implications. Following is a brief list of details to consider when making a list of people you might want to ask to serve in this capacity:

- ☐ **Eligibility:** Different states have different rules about **eligibility**; it is best to consult legal counsel to understand New Jersey's procedures, although one could proceed without an attorney. If you move, be sure to check whether your named guardians are still allowed to serve.

- ☐ **Common ideals:** People who have similar views about child rearing, values, and religious beliefs are more likely to raise your children or care for your adult family members the way you would.

- ☐ **Compassionate:** There could be a need to address the emotional and practical issues and needs that come up as a result of your death.

☐ **Flexible:** Different people react differently to dramatic changes in life, so it might be necessary for the guardian to take time off work or move to a new home to be available to address the needs of his or her charge.

☐ **Emotional stability:** Grief is a reasonable response to death, but a person who is prone to depression or has mental health issues might be unable to care for others during such a critical time.

☐ **Marital status:** Some people prefer that children have a two-parent family; others are more focused on the personality of the guardian, and maybe being single means being more flexible. Consider what is most important to you, and be true to that criterion.

☐ **Location:** If the guardian is unable to move into your home or be close to his or her adult charge, those entrusted to them might have to move, and that could create additional stresses for already-stressed people.

Things to keep in mind:

- Some family members might be unhappy with your choice of guardian or might believe they are the best choice. Be prepared to address fears, concerns, and frustrations — even anger — with those who disagree with your choices.

- Always discuss the expectations and responsibilities with the potential guardian before naming that person in a will or other legal document.

- If it makes you both feel more comfortable, spell out your expectations for each guardian in writing so that you are both clear about your wishes.

- Always choose secondary and tertiary guardians in the event that unexpected situations (your first choice dies before you do) or life circumstances (serious illness or a job transfer to another country) make it impossible for that person to agree to be a guardian.

- Be aware that the court might decide that your choices for a guardian is unsuitable — maybe your brother was recently arrested on drunken-driving charges — and choose another guardian based on what the judge thinks is in the best interest of the child or person in need of a guardian. In these situations naming secondary and tertiary guardians can be helpful in guiding the court.

Executor

Just as you need to carefully select your guardians, you need to consider who will manage the affairs of your estate, as opposed to running off to the Cayman Islands with everything in your trust funds.

See Chapter 5 for more information on the responsibilities of an executor. The following list offers a quick summary of his or her duties:

- Guiding your will through the probate process to make sure it is accepted as valid. This also means defending the will against any challenges.

- Collecting your assets.

- Overseeing the transition of gifts made to beneficiaries. This might include a title transfer for a house or making sure a life insurance policy check is made out in the correct name.

- Reviewing, evaluating, and paying any claims against your estate. These commonly include taxes and outstanding bills that are owed.

- Raising the money to pay claims. This can mean selling assets, such as a house or car.

- Preparing and filing an accounting of all financial transactions for the court.

The person who takes on this task must know what is involved. For this reason, choosing a secondary executor is a good idea; if you do not appoint one, the court will appoint one for your estate.

☑ Choosing an Executor or Trustee

The choice of an executor or a trustee is a highly personal decision, so there is no cookie-cutter definition or approach. Some details to consider are:

☐ **Integrity:** Can you trust this person, no matter what?

☐ **Your relationship:** Does this person know you well enough personally and professionally to know how you think and might want things handled?

☐ **Personality:** How will this person deal with a grieving family when decisions must be made?

☐ **Thoughtfulness:** Will this person consider questions and demands made on your estate by creditors, beneficiaries, the court, or anyone contesting your will and wishes?

☐ **Common sense:** When given multiple choices, does this person tend to be practical?

☐ **Realism:** If this person does not know what to do, will he or she seek the advice of experts?

☐ **Potential conflicts of interest:** Could decisions made by this person benefit others, including your trustee/executor, and harm your family?

☐ **Asset-management skills:** What kind of experience does this person have with real estate and financial markets, for example?

☐ **Real-estate management skills:** Is this person informed about what it takes to maintain and manage property in your estate, be it a house or undeveloped piece of land?

☐ **Knowledge of beneficiaries:** Can this person accurately assess the needs of your beneficiaries without your day-to-day guidance?

☐ **Criminal background:** Has this person ever been convicted of a crime related to the responsibilities you are asking of him or her?

Additional considerations/notes

_____

_____

_____

_____

People of Influence

After you are gone, the people who will have the most influence over what happens to your estate, in the legal pecking order, are the probate court, creditors, and your beneficiaries.

Probate court judge

This section contains general information about how probate court operates. *Specifics about how probate court accepts, records, and addresses issues with wills are addressed in Chapter 11.*

Probate court is part of a state's court system; some states have special judges who only handle estate settlement cases, whereas other states might not specialize in this way. New Jersey courts are organized to handle probate proceedings through their trial court system in county surrogate courts. Regardless of the laws governing the organizational structure of the court, a probate judge will review the legal documents related to an estate. If a person dies without a will, the judge will appoint an administrator who serves in the same capacity as an executor. He or she also will ask for and review details, such as the will (if there is one), the inventory of assets, and petitions from creditors and heirs. Heir is the legal title of a person who inherits property from an estate that does not have a will, or is intestate; beneficiaries are those who receive an inheritance by being named in a legal document such as a will or trust.

The judge will supervise the process of settling an estate and will only adjudicate, or hand down decisions, as they are needed, such as when a creditor makes a claim and is denied payment by the administrator. The same can be done when a person comes forward and claims to be an heir to an estate.

The judge might choose someone you think is unsuitable for the job of administrator, and he or she might agree to pay the claim of an old business partner whom you do not feel you owe. You can prevent these items from happening by creating an estate plan and avoiding probate when possible.

Probate judges also establish guardianship and handle other special circumstances, such as bigamy, live-in lovers who want part of an estate, or "long-lost children" who contest decisions regarding heirs.

Creditors

Your debts get paid first, so how much you owe other people at the time of your death will determine how much of your estate goes to your loved ones and charities. Some creditors might not make a claim against your estate. Maybe you borrowed $5,000 from Aunt Henrietta and she does not care about being paid back, so when your executor writes a check, she simply tears it up and hands it back.

Outstanding credit card balances, a personal line of credit from a bank, and a car loan are just a few examples of the bills you might be paying when you are alive, and these must be settled after your death. In addition to letting creditors know about your passing, your executor will request the amount of payments necessary to settle your accounts. Some companies, upon reading a death notice, might try to make a claim of payments due. It is up to the executor or administrator — or the probate judge, if this becomes necessary — to determine whether a claim is legitimate and must be paid.

Beneficiaries

Even if you die intestate, which means to die without leaving a will, a number of will substitutes make it possible for your estate to avoid probate: joint ownership of property, wherein the surviving partner automatically takes full control; revocable and irrevocable trusts; life insurance, pensions, and annuities with named beneficiaries; and stocks, bonds, and bank accounts paid to a designated person upon the death of the owner.

If a beneficiary is not named — or the primary beneficiary declines the bequest, or is dead and a secondary beneficiary is not named — then the probate court judge will decide who receives the unclaimed property.

Beneficiaries and court-named heirs can challenge decisions made about an inheritance — whether you or the court makes that decision. People who believe they should have received an inheritance or who only received a fraction of what they were told they would get — or think they deserve — can challenge the will or court ruling. These challenges can hold up the resolution of your estate for months or years, so making sure your legal documents are in order can help reduce this problem.

These basic elements of an estate plan describe what is involved and who is integral to the process. Next are the components of an estate plan — the documents, accounts, and policies that make it all legal and taxable.

CASE STUDY: DETAILS AND LEGALESE DO MATTER

Scott M. Slovin, Esq.
Schwartz Manes Ruby & Slovin
sslovin@smrslaw.com
www.smrslaw.com

What are some estate-plan essentials?

The biggest concern in an estate plan is coordinating all of the estate-plan documents, such as the will, with the trust and beneficiary designations, as well as ownership of assets, including payable-on-death or transfer-on-death-type assets. Essential information includes the following:

- The name of the testator (the person preparing the will) or the grantor or settlor (the name of the person creating the trust) of the trust.
- Beneficiaries' names and relationships to the testator or the grantor, as well as alternate (contingent) beneficiaries, should a beneficiary predecease the testator or grantor.

- The fiduciaries (the executor or trustee) and the guardians for the minor children.
- How estate taxes and other expenses of the estate will be paid and from which assets the cash will be drawn.

The benefits of working with an attorney are to avoid mistakes in drafting — such as unclear bequests or failure to specify from what assets taxes will be paid — and to reduce federal and state estate taxes that a non-estate-planning lawyer or a non-attorney might fail to take into consideration.

Why is it important to use legal terms in estate-planning documents? So many of them are confusing.

There is a long history of interpretation under state law and federal tax law, and attorneys like to use language that they know has been interpreted by the courts to achieve the results they are seeking for clients. Attorneys are trying to simplify their language and create wills and trusts that are easier to read and for clients to follow.

How does a person go about choosing a professional in your field?

The best way to choose an estate-planning attorney is to seek the recommendation of financial planners, accountants, and insurance agents who work with estate-planning attorneys. Make sure you choose someone who does more than a couple of wills per year. You need to find someone who spends at least half of the time in estate planning so that he or she understands all of the nuances of state probate and estate law, as well as tax law. Especially important would be attorneys who have extra training in the field of estate planning and tax planning. Recommendations of friends and neighbors would also be important.

CHAPTER 3

Components of an Effective Estate Plan

Car keys, directions, map, water bottle, and snacks: Planning for a road trip is easy because the basics of what you need are easy to identify and collect. The car does not go anywhere without the keys, and directions are essential for reaching the final destination. Similarly, how you plan to achieve the goals of your estate planning can be equally simple, after you know the things that are necessary.

Like taking a road trip to a new place, there are plenty of guidebooks and maps prepared by those who have gone on this trip before — ranging from specialized and highly trained professionals to those who have learned from personal experience. These people can help you do the things that will make your trip unique for you, and there is no need to use much time and energy figuring it all out on your own. The components of an effective estate plan are all the same; what individualizes each plan is which pieces match your goals and how those components work together.

Much legal language is involved in estate plans, but everyday words can be used for the same things, just like a road that has a state route number (SR 56), a formal name (Lillian Paulsson Memorial Highway), and what the locals call it (Lil's Lane). Sometimes, knowing the description of something is good enough to gain the necessary understanding — "property is stuff you own," for example — so that you can find your way when the map gets confusing.

Legally Speaking

A court only recognizes legally binding documents as the way to give your estate to others. Some of these are so widely known and commonly used that descriptions and definitions hardly seem necessary; most people know what a will is and what it is for. But the difference between what makes a document truly legal, as opposed to what you think is legal, can get you into trouble: If you do not have the right wording, enough witnesses, or the right witnesses, all of your efforts can be ignored.

The following are reoccurring terms you will find throughout this book:

- **Property:** The things you own, which can be anything you want to give to other people; also referred to as principal.

- **Real property:** This is any kind of real estate.

  o **Types:** Vacant land that you buy with the intention of building on, or it might just be an investment that you plan to sell later without developing; your primary residence; a second home, such as a vacation condo; a portion of a home, such as a timeshare; investment property, such as a two-family house that you own yourself and which generates rental income; or property in which you share ownership with a partner or business.

- **Personal property:** Your possessions. This category is further divided into tangible personal property — things you can touch — and intangible personal property, or financial assets.

o **Tangible:** Jewelry, artwork, furniture, china, collectibles such as figurines or antique books, electronic equipment, cars, and boats.

o **Intangible:** Checking accounts, savings accounts, money market funds, mutual funds, stocks, bonds, or retirement accounts such as a pension, an individual retirement arrangement (IRA), a Roth IRA, or a Keogh plan.

- **Property interest:** This refers to the connection you have to a specific item, piece of land, or other belongings.

  o **Legal interest:** This is property you can legally transfer or manage but is not yours to use or keep for yourself. Someone who is responsible for the maintenance and oversight of the use of a piece of property but does not legally own it is called a trustee.

    ▶ *Example: Steve manages the house and grounds of his Great Grandmother Julie's family home because she lives in a nursing home. He calls a plumber and contracts to have work done so that the backed-up drains are fixed. Steve might even place an ad in the paper to rent the house, screen applicants, and serve as the primary contract for the renter, collecting rent and addressing problems. But the property is in Julie's name, and Steve cannot sell the house or any of the land because it belongs to her.*

  o **Beneficial interest:** You receive a benefit from the property.

    ▶ *Example: Veronica always wanted to go to art school, but she thought the tuition was too expensive, even with student loans. After she graduated from high school, her grandfather told her he had set up a trust fund for her, and*

> *the proceeds from that trust will pay her tuition and fees for art school.*

- **Ownership:** What the individual or individuals who hold the legal title to a piece of property have. The ability to retain, sell, or give away this property depends on the number of people who hold that title (in some cases, it also depends on their relationship) and any legal agreements/contracts connected to the property.

  o **Sole ownership:** A single person holds the title to the property.

    ▶ *Example: Mandy owns her car because she paid cash for it, and the title of the car is in her name.*

  o **Joint ownership:** When any two people hold an equal share of the title to a piece of property. The most common form is spousal, which is when a legally married couple has both names on a title to a piece of property.

    ▶ *Example: Joe and Mary are listed on the mortgage and the deed to the home they live in together.*

- **Community property:** A state law that views a wife and husband as equal partners and assumes a 50/50 split of ownership.

    ▶ *Example: When Clyde and Bonnie divorced, everything they owned that was not a specific gift from a family member or something owned before or after the marriage was lumped together and divided into two equal parts.*

- **Separate property:** Things that are owned by one spouse that are not part of the couple's community property.

  ▶ **Example:** *Fred owned an antique Model A before he and Carrie married, and the title is in his name.*

- **Joint tenancy:** A group of people hold equal and undivided title to a piece of property.

  ▶ **Example:** *Brian, Joseph, and Greg own a cottage together in Michigan. All their names are on the deed to the property, and they schedule their vacation time so that everyone has an opportunity to use the cottage.*

- **Exemption:** This is a specific amount of money that will not be affected by estate taxes. Federal taxes and states with an estate tax often set an amount, such as $1 million, that is tax-free. Taxes would then be due on $1,000,001 and beyond. For 2010, there was no federal estate tax. New Jersey has an estate tax, with an exemption maximum $675,000. New Jersey estate tax will be reduced by the portion of the tax that is attributable to property located outside New Jersey.

- **Donor:** The person who gives a gift or bequest.

- **Beneficiary:** The individual(s) or group(s) that will receive the property in a will or trust. This can be a single person (a nephew), a group of people (all grandchildren), one group (Stray Cat Rescue, Inc.), several groups (all community councils in your city), or a combination of any of these.

- **Distribution:** The disbursement or payment of property from an account to a beneficiary. It could be in the form of a check of some other monetary payment, or it could be the transfer of a title into the name of the beneficiary.

You will see many of these terms throughout this book, and some definitions will be expanded upon in sections that provide more detailed information.

Defining Your Estate

Understanding what property is and how ownership is determined makes it possible for you to define your estate. Making a list of what constitutes your estate and what makes up the estate of a spouse or life partner will make it easier to understand some of the choices you have for creating your own plan.

This list, combined with the fundamental values you defined in Chapter 2, will help you consider how a specific estate-planning component might be a good tool for you. There are many choices to make, and it will not be possible to make final decisions quickly, but having some information about your estate in mind while you learn can make the process go more smoothly.

Pass the Parchment

Before modern times, many important books and legal documents were printed on parchment. Only the wealthy could read, write, or afford to buy parchment for their private use or for special occasions, such as drafting the Declaration of Independence. Even though most of the documents that make up your retirement plan will not have the same historical impact as that document had, it is important to make sure the documentation you do is complete and accurate. If you forget a clause or use the wrong word, the directions you leave will not be worth the paper they are printed on.

What the document is, what it can do, and the laws affecting each will help you choose the elements of your estate plan that will transform your thoughts and wishes into action.

Will

What it is

A legal document in which you identify the people or institutions that should receive money and property from your estate after your death. It also serves to appoint guardianship of children or adults who are your legal responsibility and designate an executor to manage your estate after you die.

What it does

- It spells out your instructions and wishes for what you want done with the property you leave behind.

- Your affairs go from being private to public when you use a will because it becomes a part of public record — if you want privacy, keep your will basic and legal. *For more information on this, see Chapter 5.*

The laws that matter

- State laws govern the execution of the instructions in a will.

- A will can be challenged and directions contained within it overturned by a judge.

Potential problems

- Thinking a will is unnecessary or is all you need. Each extreme limits your estate plan's effectiveness.

- Using a will form from the grocery store or the Internet. Unless you know the laws of New Jersey and how the language of that document matches up, you could have a false sense of security about what will happen after your death.

Will substitute

What it is

An agreement, contract, or other legal arrangement that accomplishes the same goals of a will — to protect and transfer property rights — but without the use of a will document. Some options are:

- Holding property in a living trust or joint tenancy.

- Payable-on-death account — the ownership of a monetary account, like a savings account, which is set up to automatically transfer the ownership of the beneficiary upon the death of the donor.

- Financial arrangements that have a named beneficiary — life insurance, IRAs, or pension plans.

What it does

- These arrangements can save time because the ownership automatically transfers to the beneficiary upon the death of the donor, so it skips the probate process.

- Privacy is preserved, again, because the substitute does not go through probate and is not subject to open-records laws.

- A substitute will can also save money because probate court fees are not needed, and some estate taxes can be avoided.

- An unconventional situation — such as multiple ex-spouses and blended families with children from previous marriages — might be better addressed with a will substitute.

The laws that matter

- Tax laws of New Jersey and the federal government; there is a significant amount of misinformation about what is tax-exempt and what is not.

Potential problems

- Missing details — each form of will substitute has its own quirks and legal requirements; not having enough signatures, witnesses, or clauses could nullify the entire document. Using the wrong language can also submarine your efforts.

- Find a qualified professional to help you close all the holes in your documents.

Trust

What it is

A legal arrangement that involves the transfer of property from the original owner to a person or company. The trust holds and maintains the property for the benefit of a specific individual, group of people, or institution(s).

What it does

The legal arrangement will hold any property in a tax-free account until distributions are made to people or institutions other than the donor, depending on the kind of trust and the beneficiary, or until the entire trust is turned over to a beneficiary.

The laws that matter

- Taxes, again. Some trusts are tax-exempt; some taxes must be paid by the beneficiary when distributions are made, or the ownership of the trust changes from your name to the beneficiary.

Be sure to know what the tax implications are — not all trusts are created equal.

- Exemptions also apply here — trusts for education, a spouse, and for other reasons can eliminate taxes in the distribution or transfer of a trust.

Potential problems

- Choosing a trust that will not achieve the results you want. Many sales reps will make a commission off the trust you establish, so they might be looking at how to maximize their profit.

- Thinking a trust is all you need.

Insurance

What it is

A method of protecting valuables in the form of a policy in which premiums are paid over time to guarantee a specific payment for a specific purpose by the company accepting the premiums. Those valuables can be property — home, car, jewelry — a person's life, or the ability to work and care for yourself — life, disability, health care, long-term care.

What it does

- These various policies protect an estate from the devastation an unexpected accident or terrible illness can bring to your finances. They can preserve your assets and allow you to spend/distribute them as you choose.

- For a small investment, insurance can dramatically increase the value of your estate.

- Some insurance policies only pay a percentage amount — long-term disability might only replace 50 percent of your pre-disability income — so what you receive depends on another factor, like your income.

The laws that matter

- Taxes, again. Know what insurance income is taxable — disability insurance payments, death benefits, and other kinds of insurance might be subject to local, state, and federal income taxes or estate taxes, depending on the age of the beneficiary.

Potential problems

- Buying more insurance than you can afford; once you stop paying premiums, the policy will no longer pay benefits.

- Believing that buying insurance is all the estate planning you need to do.

Taxes

What they are

Estate taxes are fees levied by federal and state governments against property that is left behind after a person dies. Gift taxes are fees levied by federal and state governments against property that is transferred to someone before the owner dies.

What they do

Taxes affect the amount of money your beneficiaries do or do not receive, because all bills, including taxes, get paid out before your beneficiaries see a dime. Carefully investigate what taxes must be paid on the property you leave behind and who is responsible for paying them.

The laws that matter

- There are all kinds of loopholes that were created and filled over the years, so federal and state tax codes in particular can be extremely confusing. It is impossible to provide a specific list.

- This is where a professional is essential to avoid fines, late fees, and other charges on top of the taxes already owed.

Potential problems

- Thinking that you will not have to pay any taxes after you die. You might not be around to write the check, but that does not stop the government from sending a bill.

- A failure to leave instructions for your executor about money you set aside specifically for the purpose of paying your estate's taxes could result in the sale of assets or other mistakes in the management of your affairs.

- An executor's failing to file your final income tax and the necessary estate tax forms can have serious consequences for your executor and the bequests you want others to receive.

Retirement funds/pension

What it is

Money saved in different kinds of accounts with the intention of using those funds to pay for living expenses after a person is no longer employed full-time. There are employer-sponsored accounts — profit-sharing plan, stock bonus plan, employee stock ownership plan (ESOP), and 401(k); individual accounts — IRA, Roth IRA, annuity, variable annuity, and Keogh plan; and government benefits in the form of social security retirement benefits, Medicare, and disability.

What it does

- Funds saved for retirement are supposed to make it possible for seniors to live comfortably without working, but planning and the right kind of saving are essential to achieving that goal.

- There are no guarantees: Just because you save does not mean the money will be there. As more companies renege on retirement plans and underfund employer pension contributions, the retirement you think you will have might not be possible.

The laws that matter

- There are serious financial penalties imposed on funds removed from retirement accounts before you reach retirement age.

- Social security benefits are taxed as income.

Potential problems

- Believing that government benefits will be enough to live on when you retire.

- Pension plans that are not insured might not deliver the benefits promised.

In the end, your estate plan might look similar to that of your spouse, or it could be completely different. It all depends on the components you value most and how you handle financial matters. Here is a bumper-sticker summary of how your estate plan might look:

"Fly first class; your kids will, after you are gone."
Ferdie and Lilly, married 65 years with three grown,
independent daughters

Will: Separate wills written at the same time, leaving everything to the surviving spouse with specific bequests of heirlooms to family and sentimental tokens to friends, with everything else going to the church in which they were married after both are gone.

Living will: Instructions to not use any extraordinary life-sustaining efforts should they experience a loss of brain function or a disease that impairs their ability to make sound decisions.

Life insurance: One policy was already cashed out to pay for an Alaskan cruise. A second policy will be used to pay for funeral expenses for the first who dies, and the last policy will be used for the survivor.

Pension plan: Spending the dividends every month; whatever is left goes into the travel fund.

Living trust: Spending the dividends every month and using the rest for road trips.

Charitable trust: All property is held in trust for the church and the animal rescue and shelter.

"Yours, Mine, and Mine."
Andrea, divorced with no children and living single
for more than 40 years

Will: Does not have one; Andrea lives on a houseboat that she rents, and all her possessions fit into whatever car she leases, so there is nothing to bequest.

Living will: Does not have one.

Life insurance: Three policies — one for Mom, one for Dad, and one for all death-related expenses.

Disability insurance: Short-term, long-term, and extended-care insurance policies.

Retirement accounts: Her 401(k), Roth IRA, and stock bonus plans will cover her monthly expenses, and whatever is left goes into a rainy-day account.

Trust: Her cabin and land she owns on Whidbey Island in Washington, where she plans to retire.

"The one with the most toys wins!"
John Richard Greenman, XIV, and Maya E. Primwater,
not married but living together for 18 years,
no children — his and hers estate planning

John Richard Greenman, XIV

Will: Fifty percent of everything not in trust goes to Maya; there is just enough information in the will to make it legally binding and uncontestable.

Living will: Instructions on how to use or refrain from using any and all extraordinary life-sustaining efforts. In New Jersey, this instrument is called a "living will" or "advanced declaration."

Life insurance: Multiple policies with multiple beneficiaries, including parents, siblings, long-time family servants, and a few elderly female relatives.

Retirement accounts: All set to roll over into trust funds to support the educational efforts of all subsequent generations of nieces and nephews, contingent upon achieving specific grade point averages, with financial rewards for exceeding those levels.

Living trust: Spending the dividends every month on lavish parties, resort vacations, and redoing the summer house in the Hamptons.

Charitable remainder trust: Several specific charities get the "leftovers," which will be approximately $11 million.

Social security: Benefits will go to support arts organizations.

Maya E. Primwater

Will: 50 percent of everything not in trust goes to "Johnny," with just enough information in the will to make it legally binding and uncontestable.

Living will: Instructions to use no extraordinary life-sustaining efforts.

Life insurance: Multiple policies with multiple beneficiaries including siblings, lifelong friends, and charities.

Retirement accounts: All set to roll over into an endowment fund to provide ongoing support for more than two dozen charities and nonprofits for which Maya volunteers.

Living trust: Spending the dividends every month on visits to overseas nonprofit organizations doing research for her endowment.

Education trust funds: Several funds are set up to send her nieces and nephews, cousins, and the children of close friends to study abroad; other funds are set up for "self-study" for those who want to find their way in a less academic environment.

Social security: Benefits will go to support local social justice groups.

Whatever money is left in her retirement accounts is to be placed in a trust after her death to establish a writers' retreat that will be operated by the Write on the Sound Writer's Conference.

By looking over these hypothetical estate plans, you can begin to see how the things you value might impact the decisions you make.

• *Did You Know?* •

The person who will eventually administer your estate has some basic guidelines to follow due to state and federal laws regarding this task. Specific taxes must be paid by certain deadlines. An extension can be granted, but only if the paperwork is completed in a certain way, submitted to the correct office, and signed by a specific person or judge. You can help make this process flow a little more smoothly by keeping that in mind and planning for some potential problems.

☑ Watch Out for This

☐ Prepare a letter with details about how to administer your estate.

☐ Provide as much detailed information as possible about your estate. Annual updates to your documents will mean fewer undocumented items for the executor to track down.

☐ Bonding requirements for your executor can be waived if you include language in your will to that effect. If your executor is a bank, you might want to keep those in place, but for a family member, this might not be necessary.

☐ Death notices must be published. Do some research about the content and method of distribution New Jersey requires and provide your executor with a list of resources and samples.

Your executor should be aware of the following items:

☐ Publish the death notices properly to avoid disputes.

☐ Be diligent in identifying and inventorying assets; an apparent lack of effort can result in legal trouble.

☐ Ask questions about anything that is unclear in legal documents and estate administration instructions, and get clarification in writing. This can help avoid potential disputes or help address those that do arise.

Details neither of you control

☐ Disputes raised by creditors or dissatisfaction about how a claim is settled.

☐ Disagreements between and challenges brought by beneficiaries.

☐ Claims made by a spouse against an estate that conflict with the terms of a will; some states entitle a spouse to a specific percentage of an estate regardless of the decedent's wishes.

CASE STUDY: COMPONENTS OF AN EFFECTIVE ESTATE PLAN

Anne Marie Griffith, Tom Kotick
SS&G Financial Services, Inc.
Certified Public Accountants and Advisers
tkotidk@ssandg.com

What is essential to include in an estate plan?

Estate planning is the process of developing and implementing a master plan that facilitates the distribution of your property after your death according to your goals and objectives.

The critical pieces involved in estate planning involve the following documents: a will; a trust in the case of minor children, a large estate, or second marriage with children from prior marriages; durable powers of attorney; a living will and a medical power of attorney or medical proxy; and a letter of instructions also is recommended. Other critical priorities of the estate-planning process involve the selection of an executor/executrix for your will/estate, a guardian for your minor children, and trustees or co-trustees in the case of any trusts created. Finally, a cash-flow analysis and some income-tax planning should be part of the priority list for the estate-planning playbook.

Anyone with property or minor children should have a will. While most people think of the will as the driving factor determining where your property goes, beneficiary designations and the titling of assets often play a bigger role in this determination. For example, when someone owns property as joint tenants with rights of survivorship, this property will go to the joint owner, regardless of what a will says. Also, many assets are governed by beneficiary designations, such as retirement plans and life insurance. These types of assets will always pass by way of the beneficiary designation, not according to a person's will.

Life insurance is one of the biggest players in the estate-planning game. For some, it is the only way to ensure that family members will be able to support themselves after the death of the primary wage earner. For those with larger estates, life insurance can provide the funds needed to pay estate taxes (and other costs) without liquidating estate assets. For those with a business interest, life insurance can be used as a vehicle for business succession. Finally, for those with a generous spirit, life insurance can permit them, to make charitable gifts.

What are the most common mistakes people make? What do people forget to include?

A very common mistake is not addressing the estate-planning process at all, which can result in what is called "dying intestate," or dying without a will. In that case, the distribution of the estate and the care of minor children are resolved by the state.

Another oversight is not funding the estate to properly care for your spouse, minor, or school-aged children in terms of ongoing financial needs for daily living and future educational costs.

Other common mistakes or oversights are in the need for annual income-tax filings for any trusts that have been created, or gift-tax return filings in the case of gifts over the annual exclusion amount.

What are the benefits of working with someone in your field?

A CPA who is experienced in working with clients on their personal financial plans, which include estate planning, can help avoid the mistakes and oversights mentioned previously.

The CPA can "quarterback" the estate-planning process. This is done in several ways, including assisting the attorney in drafting the documents in accordance with the client's needs and desires, as well as recommending a good estate attorney if the client does not enter the process with an attorney; coordinating the work of the investment/

broker to properly identify and re-title assets; and working with the life insurance agent to make sure ongoing living and educational expenses are covered with the right amount and type of life insurance coverage and policy.

The CPA is usually involved in the preparation of any annual trust or gift-tax filing requirements that might spring from the planning process. The CPA will gather the information necessary to make the filings by coordinating the assistance and necessary input from other team members to make the proper filings each year.

How does a person go about choosing a professional in your field?

If a client is working with a CPA for his annual personal and/or business accounting and tax work, you can start by asking if he or she does estate planning as well as income taxes. Or you can ask your CPA for a referral to a CPA who is experienced in the financial-planning process involving estate planning.

It helps qualify the CPA if he or she has certain additional certifications, such as the PFS (Personal Financial Specialist) designation, or a CFP® (Certified Financial Planner®). Also helpful is a CPA who has studied for and retains a state life-insurance license.

CHAPTER 4

Taxes

When Roman Emperor Caesar Augustus was running short on cash to pay for things like aqueducts and parties, he created the first estate levy. Ever since then, death and taxes have been linked. Unfortunately, our version of that original tax law has become complicated and confusing over time.

When one loophole is discovered, a new rule is created to cover it. But then that rule has a little wiggle room that needs to be closed up, so another rule is created — and the cycle continues. So do not count on an easy answer to the question of how much tax money your estate will have to pay after you die. Your best bet is to track down people who specialize in tax law — a CPA or an attorney.

The gross estate, which is the value of all property owned by the deceased person on the date of death, is what gets taxed. The federal government gets a chunk based on the Estate Recovery Act — the estate tax, referred to as the "death tax" by those in Congress who want to completely do away with it. Some states have a state estate tax similar to that of the federal government, though other states levy a tax on the property received by the beneficiary — an inheritance tax. All these taxes have a host of exemptions or deductions that reduce or eliminate the taxes that need to be paid.

Strategically using the exemptions and deductions and also creating tax-free accounts makes it possible to get around some of these taxes. That is one of the best benefits of estate planning. Before you can save taxes, you need to know what they are and how much you might owe. Without a crystal ball or clairvoyance, it is impossible to know what the precise worth of your estate will be at the time of your death, but planning for what you do know puts you in a position to help your loved ones avoid some painful tax bills.

Keep in mind that no matter how much you prepare, tax laws can change with the stroke of a pen in Washington, D.C., or Trenton, and everything you thought you knew and planned for can change. Consider all the information in this section to be accompanied by an asterisk, which means subject to change at any time; do not consider this information to be the definitive legal authority.

Check with a tax professional who is current with federal and state-tax law changes.

Federal First

There are three federal taxes that directly affect your estate: the gift tax, the generation-skipping transfer tax, and the estate tax. Bear in mind that these federal tax schemes are in flux as of 2010 and are subject to further legislation.

Generally, any gift you give to another person or institution — in cash or the transfer of property — in one fiscal year is subject to a gift tax. There is an exemption: The first $13,000 given to any single person or organization is exempt from the tax, but everything from $13,001 and beyond is subject to gift taxation.

► **Example:** *You decide to give your niece Meghan $5,000 as a high school graduation present because she wants to tour Europe before going to college.*

No. Because this gift is under $13,000, you do not owe any taxes on this gift.

You can only give Meghan another $8,000 this year and have it be tax-free. If you make the next gift $9,000, you will owe the gift tax on $1,000.

As the donor, the person who gives a gift, you are eligible for some tax deductions that might also make the tax bill go away. The donee, the person or institution receiving the gift, is what determines the deduction or exclusion you can apply:

Tax deductions — your spouse, many charities
Exclusions — medical expenses, political organizations, tuition

► **Example:** *Your husband has an opportunity to buy a workshop full of woodworking tools from an elderly neighbor who is giving up the hobby. He has his own checking account, but it was his turn to add money to the children's college fund this month and he does not have enough cash. So, you give him the money from your checking account.*

No. The marital tax deduction means you can give your spouse $150,000 a year and it is tax-free.

If you try to do the same thing with the man you have lived with for 18 years and are not married to, you will have to pay the gift tax on $137,000. You still get to take advantage of the annual $13,000 exemption.

Like most things, these deductions and exclusions all have fine print. To have an unlimited, tax-free marital deduction, your spouse must be married and a U.S. citizen at the time the gift is made.

▶ **Example:** *It is Friday night, and your grandson Thomas calls, absolutely frantic. His tuition is due the following week, and he cannot reach Mom (she is out of state at a convention). Dad has not been around for years — and even if he were, he almost certainly would not have the $13,200 he owes. You write down the name of the school, address, and all of the particulars so that you can have your bank transfer the funds on Monday.*

No. For the education exclusion to be on the up-and-up, the gift must be paid directly to the educational institution, so you will not owe any taxes.

The education exclusion is for tuition or training only. Thomas is on his own for books, unless you give him additional cash.

When it comes to charities, they must be qualified by the Internal Revenue Service (IRS). You cannot just give money to an animal shelter and deduct that from your taxes; you have to make sure the IRS has recognized the entity as a charity, called a 501c3 designation, and the gifts you give to a charity need to fit into predetermined categories:

- This is property that you give to a charity without getting anything in return. The gift can be cash or any other type of property.

- The sale of a piece of property to a charity at a rate that is below the fair market value. The difference between the amount paid and the actual value is the amount of the gift.

- The transfer of stock ownership from your name to that of the charity. The fair market value of the stock at the time of the transfer is the gift amount.

Many other conditions that must be met to make your gift tax-free, regardless of who gets the gift. That is why you must consult with a tax expert to make sure your interpretation of your gift matches what the government allows. Unless you are a whiz at tax law, you are in all probability going to need some help navigating the ever-changing federal estate tax.

In 2001, a law called the Economic Growth and Tax Relief Reconciliation Act was passed that increased the exemption for the estate tax. In 2002 and 2003, taxes were owed on anything over $1 million. So, if your estate was worth $1.5 million, you only had to pay tax on $500,000. At a 45 percent tax rate — the highest federal tax rate for an estate — the exemptions create a limit to the money the feds can collect. The exemption increased to $3.5 million until 2009, then the tax was repealed in 2010 until 2011, when the exemption is expected to go back down to $1 million — unless Congress steps in and repeals the tax for good or makes some other determination for the taxing scheme. The estates of several billionaires who have passed away in 2010 have benefitted from the 2010 reprieve.

For a while, some people managed to dodge the estate tax dilemma. A person with a multimillion-dollar estate did not want to have less money to give to her beneficiaries, so she named her grandchildren or great-grandchildren as the beneficiaries. They are all minors, so they do not have to pay any taxes on their inheritance. However, the federal government caught on to that and created a tax specifically designed to tax the money skipping over generations. Called the Generation-Skipping Tax Transfer (GSTT), it is the most complex tax law, according to the experts in the field.

Entire books have been written about this topic, and they still do not encompass all the details. Suffice it to say, if your estate is worth more than

$1 million (for expected federal purpose, $675,000 in New Jersey), you are well-advised to work with an estate-tax planner to make sure you consider all the implications of trying to give all your worldly goods to the youngest of your family tree.

• *Did You Know?* •

Children under the age of 14 are required to pay income tax at the single-person tax rate on income earned through employment. They must file a tax return like everyone else, but they get special treatment by the IRS if their parents are wealthy and try to give a large sum of money.

"Kiddie tax" is the term used to describe income tax applied to money that minors did not earn through employment, also called unearned income. In 1996, a special law was created to close a loophole that allowed parents to give their children a large gift as a way to pay a lower tax on the interest earned. The child tax rate was significantly lower than the adult rate.

The law has changed over the years, and in 2008, it changed again. The first $900 in income made on any investment in a child's name — age 19 and younger, extending to the age of 24 if the child is in school full time — is not subject to income tax. The next $900 is subject to a 10 percent tax, up to $90. Anything above $1,800 is taxed at the tax rate of the child's parent(s).

☑ Watch Out for This

- ☐ You can take advantage of your child's lower income-tax bracket by investing in U.S. Savings Bonds. The income is deferred, and so are the taxes.

- ☐ Money paid to your child in the form of wages for working in your business is not subject to the "kiddie tax." Those payments are deductible by your business, but it is important to keep the necessary records for hours and work performed. Not having these could make it appear as though you are trying to cheat on your business taxes.

☐ A child earning his or her own income and paying taxes can still be declared as a dependent on a parent's tax return, allowing that parent to take a standard deduction. If you divorce and do not get custody of the children, you do not get "custody" of the standard deduction for your taxes.

Now for the State

The state wants to get some of that estate you are leaving behind, too. Some states copied the federal law, and others, like New Jersey, have created a state estate tax, which means your estate has to pay taxes on the property you leave behind.

Other states levy a tax on the property received by a beneficiary — an inheritance tax. New Jersey imposes a graduated inheritance tax on property transfers greater than $500. Exempt from inheritance tax are surviving spouses, domestic partners, and civil union partners, as well as the decedent's parents, grandparents, children, adopted children, stepchildren, and grandchildren. As shown by New Jersey's approach, most states with inheritance tax typically exempt closely related beneficiaries of the deceased or levy a lower tax. For example, a brother usually has a larger exemption or rate levied than a distant cousin.

Some states also impose a state gift tax. To find out whether your state has such a tax, whether there is an annual exclusion, lifetime exemptions for close family members, or for any other legal technicalities, a good place to begin is the state's department of taxation. New Jersey does not levy a gift tax unless the gift is given in anticipation of death, which is presumed if given within three years of death.

Then, there is the state income tax on income earned or received during the tax year prior to death. You can be a full- or part-time resident, or simply live in the state for a few months out of the year, but not officially be registered as a part-time resident. Income earned in another state might be taxable in New Jersey. Any inheritance you receive that counts as income and is entered on your federal tax form might also be taxed unless personal exemptions apply.

Finally, some states also tax intangible property — bonds, stocks, accounts receivable, and patents. Giving any of those things from your estate to a family member or friend before or after you die could result in a tax for the recipient. New Jersey includes intangible property under its inheritance tax scheme.

Mistakes Happen ... Frequently

The only federal regulation that might be more complex than tax law is immigration law. This complexity is why people make costly mistakes, miss savings opportunities, and wind up confused about what can and cannot be done legally. Most tax specialists are CPAs or lawyers, and it is their job to stay ahead of the latest changes to the ever-growing tax code.

Over time, some common mistakes related to taxes and estate planning have emerged. This list is a sample of those errors; it can help you identify holes in your own planning, help you prepare for a meeting with a tax advisor, and, at the very least, inspire you not to get careless about managing this element of your own estate plan.

Mistakes your executor can make include:

- Using the wrong IRS forms when filing taxes. This can involve consulting the wrong tables and filling out and submitting the wrong schedule — like using the 1040 EZ income tax form when, by law, you are required to use the 1040 long form.

- Missing information about your estate. If you do not provide or disclose all the information, your executor might not know about an account that is taxable, making him or her liable for any oversight that occurs. The "But he didn't tell me" defense will not work.

- Not having the necessary record to justify or back up the filing. This can mean having no mileage record, and missing receipts and account interest statements.

- Preparing a return without professional help. Professionals who are up-to-date on all the current tax laws can help an executor avoid a multitude of mistakes, such as using the wrong form or having insufficient documentation.

- Miscalculations. This can involve transposing numbers or just coming up with the wrong number when adding or subtracting.

- Not signing the tax form.

Decision-making mistakes you can make while preparing an estate plan:

- When to bequeath a gift: before or after death

- How to use gifts that fall below the annual gift-tax exclusion amount ($13,000 for 2010)

- The most advantageous way to structure a life insurance policy

- Selecting a trust with the maximum tax advantages for you and the beneficiary

- When it is best to leave property to a spouse

- Whether to make a bequest that will negatively impact the tax position of the beneficiary

If you want to look up a specific topic or try your hand at sorting the rules related to a specific estate-planning element — such as trusts — refer to www.irs.gov.

When, Not If, You Pay

The No. 1 benefit many professionals cite for estate planning is dramatically reducing the amount of taxes that will be paid out of your estate. However, the only way to accomplish that is to know the tax laws of New Jersey, the tax requirements of any state in which you own property, and the tax implications of the way you choose to save and distribute your estate.

The federal estate tax rate begins at 45 percent and goes as high as 50 percent. It is best to check where those rates stand every time you review or change your estate plan to make sure you have enough money available to cover the bill, if you are not going to leave that job to your loved ones. You can put a provision in your will to pick up any taxes for your beneficiaries if you want to, but a lawyer will have to help you with the wording to make that possible.

It is the job of the executor of your estate to handle all these money matters. In addition to calculating the value of your estate, she must file a tax return for your estate, called the fiduciary return, with the IRS and make the necessary payments, if there are any.

There is a deadline for paying an estate tax — it cannot just be paid whenever your executor gets around to it. That deadline is regularly 90 days after the date of death, but sometimes arrangements can be made for special circumstances.

In 2010, you did not have to worry about estate tax. Beginning in 2011, an estate of $1 million or more might be taxable unless Congress does something different with present law. New Jersey still has the estate/inheritance/gift tax scheme to consider. The best way to avoid taxes is to leave your entire estate to your spouse, a charity, or some combination thereof.

Your executor has a few options for saving some tax money, but this is where advice from an estate professional is crucial. If your executor does the wrong thing, it will cost him personally. Your executor should consider the following:

- Be sure all possible deductions are included in the fiduciary return; these include funeral expenses, expenses to your estate (e.g., appraisal fees or probate court costs), debts (e.g., mortgage or credit cards), charitable contributions, and marital deductions. The marital deduction can only be taken if your spouse is a U.S. citizen.

- Value the assets of the estate at a later date as opposed to right at death. This can only be done under the correct circumstances, and whether it is a beneficial move depends upon the individual estate and time of death.

- Income going into the estate can be manipulated to the advantage of the estate. Timing the sale of property or sending out requests for payments due can be scheduled to the advantage of filing the deceased's last income tax return and the fiduciary return the executor must file for the estate.

- Estate distributions to beneficiaries also can be timed so that the beneficiary must pay the tax, not the estate: If the payments to beneficiaries are made before the fiduciary return is filed, then the estate's value drops, making the taxes due also drop.

Your beneficiaries can also reduce their tax bills by declining to accept a bequest. Federal and state tax laws permit a disclaimer, which is a refusal to accept a gift. Whether this is a single beneficiary or joint bequest, one or both parties can decline, but it must be refused in writing, commonly within nine months of your death.

There are choices you can make in your estate planning before others need to make decisions about how to handle the taxes on your estate. When properly coordinated, some choices create an opportunity to reduce the potential tax burden on your estate and beneficiaries. These are some ways to reduce taxes, so it is a good idea to keep these in the back of your mind while working on your complete estate plan:

- Make gifts before you die to reduce your estate's value.

- Put property into tax-free trusts. *See Chapter 6 for more information about your choices.*

- Schedule property transfers to take place at the time of your death.

- Coordinate your estate planning with your spouse and divvy up assets to the best advantage for both of you.

- Use permissible exemptions, such as leaving your entire estate to your spouse.

- Consider investing in life insurance and structuring the policies carefully. *See Chapter 7 for more information on how this works with life insurance.*

However, like all estate-planning decisions, choosing the wrong options or not using the right language can lay waste to all your careful planning. Do not try this on your own.

• *Did You Know?* •

The fees paid to an executor as compensation for the time he or she puts into managing and closing out your estate are taxable income. If your executor opts not to accept a fee, then the money you designate for that purpose becomes part of your estate. If it is not held in a tax-free account, that money can be subject to estate tax.

☑ Watch Out for This

☐ Talk to your executor about a fee. If your executor does not want to be compensated, then you can plan accordingly.

CASE STUDY: TAX ADVICE FROM THE IRS

Internal Revenue Service (IRS)
1-800-829-1040
Hours of operation: Monday - Friday,
7 a.m. - 10 p.m. your local time
(Alaska & Hawaii follow Pacific Time)
www.irs.gov

The IRS is the ultimate source for all things related to taxation. Its website offers extensive resources for those who wish to learn more about anything related to taxes. What follows is a copy of the frequently asked questions (FAQ) on the Estate Taxes page. The IRS is not in the habit of helping people figure out how to reduce their tax bills, but it will give you all you need to know to be "legal." Simply achieving the goal of compliance with tax law is not something even the FAQ can guarantee. The recurring qualifiers and other sources you need to check make it clear that dealing with estate taxes on your own is risky.

When can I expect the Estate Tax Closing Letter?

There can be some variation, but for returns that are accepted as filed and contain no other errors or special circumstances, you should expect to wait about four to six months after the return is filed to receive your closing letter. Returns that are selected for examination or reviewed for statistical purposes will take longer.

What is included in the estate?

The gross estate of the decedent consists of an accounting of everything you own or have certain interests in at the date of death. The fair market value of these items is used, not necessarily what you paid for them or what their values were when you acquired them. The total of all of these items is your gross estate. The includible property may consist of cash and securities, real estate, insurance, trusts, annuities, business interests, and other assets. Keep in mind that the gross estate will likely include nonprobate, as well as probate, property.

I own a half interest in a farm (or building or business) with my brother (sister, friend, other). What is included?

Depending on how your half interest is held and treated under state law — and how it was acquired — you would probably only include half of its value in your gross estate. However, many other factors influence this answer, so you would need to visit with a tax or legal professional to make that determination.

What is excluded from the estate?

Generally, the gross estate does not include property owned solely by the decedent's spouse or other individuals. Lifetime gifts that are complete (no powers or other control over the gifts are retained) are not included in the gross estate (but taxable gifts are used in the computation of the estate tax). Life estates given to the decedent by others in which the decedent has no further control or power at the date of death are not included.

What deductions are available to reduce the estate tax?

1. Marital deduction: One of the primary deductions for married decedents is the marital deduction. All property that is included in the gross estate and passes to the surviving spouse is eligible for the marital deduction. The property must pass "outright." In some cases, certain life estates also qualify for the marital deduction.

2. Charitable deduction: If the decedent leaves property to a qualifying charity, it is deductible from the gross estate.

3. Mortgages and debt.

4. Administration expenses of the estate.

5. Losses during estate administration.

What other information do I need to include with the return?

Among other items listed:

1. Copies of the death certificate

2. Copies of the decedent's will and/or relevant trusts

3. Copies of appraisals

4. Copies of relevant documents regarding litigation involving the estate

5. Documentation of any unusual items shown on the return (partially included assets, losses, near-date-of-death transfers, others)

What is "fair market value?"

Fair market value is defined as "the price at which the property would change hands between a willing buyer and a willing seller, neither being under any compulsion to buy or to sell, and both having reasonable knowledge of relevant facts. The fair market value of a particular item of property includible in the decedent's gross estate is not to be determined by a forced sale price. Nor is the fair market value of an item of property to be determined by the sale price of the item in a market other than that in which such item is most commonly sold to the public, taking into account the location of the item wherever appropriate."

What about the value of my family business/farm?

Generally, the fair market value of such interests owned by the decedent are includible in the gross estate at date of death. However, for certain farms or businesses operated as a family farm or business, reductions to these amounts may be available.

In the case of a qualifying family farm, IRC §2032A allows a reduction from value of up to $820,000.

If the decedent owned an interest in a qualifying family-owned business, a deduction from the gross estate in the amount of up to $1.1 million may be available under IRC §2057.

What if I do not have everything ready for filing by the due date?

The estate's representative may request an extension of time to file for up to six months from the due date of the return. However, the correct amount of tax is still due by the due date, and interest is accrued on any amounts still owed by the due date that are not paid at that time.

Whom should I hire to represent me and prepare and file the return?

The IRS cannot make recommendations about specific individuals, but following are several factors to consider:

1. How complex is the estate? By the time most estates reach $1 million, there is usually some complexity involved.
2. How large is the estate?
3. In what condition are the decedent's records?
4. How many beneficiaries are there, and are they cooperative?
5. Do I need an attorney, CPA, enrolled agent (EA), or other professional(s)?

With these questions in mind, it is a good idea to discuss the matter with several attorneys and CPAs or EAs. Ask about how much experience they have had, and ask for referrals. This process should be similar to locating a good physician. Locate other individuals who have had similar experiences and ask for recommendations. Finally, after the individual(s) are employed and begin to work on estate matters, make sure the lines of communication remain open so that there are no surprises during administration or if the estate tax return is examined.

Finally, most estates engage the services of both attorneys and CPAs or EAs. The attorney usually handles probate matters and reviews the impact of documents on the estate tax return. The CPA or EA often handles the actual return preparation and some representation of the estate in matters with the IRS. However, some attorneys handle all the work. CPAs and EAs may also handle most of the work, but cannot take care of probate matters and other situations in which a law license is required. In addition, other professionals (such as appraisers, surveyors, financial advisors and others) may need to be engaged during this time.

Do I have to talk to the IRS during an examination?

You do not have to be present during an examination unless an IRS representative needs to ask specific questions. Although you may represent yourself during an examination, most executors prefer that professional(s) they have employed handle this phase of administration. They may delegate authority for this by signing a designation on the Form 706 itself, or executing Form 2848, "Power of Attorney."

What if I disagree with the examination proposals?

You have many rights and avenues of appeal if you disagree with any proposals made by the IRS.

What happens if I sell property that I have inherited?

The sale of such property is usually considered the sale of a capital asset and may be subject to capital gains (or loss) treatment. However, IRC §1014 provides that the basis of property acquired from a decedent is its fair market value at the date of death, so there is usually little or no gain to account for if the sale occurs soon after the date of death. Remember, the rules are different for determining the basis of property received as a lifetime gift.

Death is big business for the federal government

The federal government is the first beneficiary to get a share of your estate, or any estate in the union. The IRS creates numerous statistics for everything it does, including tracking the number of deaths by state, the number of estates that pay taxes, and the amount of taxes paid. Part of that information is listed below to give a sense of just how much money was added to the coffers of the U.S. government.

These numbers are in the thousands of dollars. After you add the zeros, you might find a new source of motivation for doing your planning now so that your family does not have to pay later.

Estate Tax Returns Filed for 2004 Decedents, by State of Residence

[All figures are estimates based on a sample — money amounts are in thousands of dollars.]

State of Residence	Gross estate, tax purposes [1]		Net estate tax	
	Number	Amount	Number	Amount
Total	42,239	185,921,379	19,294	22,219,722
Alabama	409	1,582,888	186	192,473
Alaska	31	99,483	* 4	* 3,739
Arizona	621	2,408,320	302	311,565
Arkansas	265	974,431	108	117,256
California	8,464	34,208,317	3,782	4,131,248
Colorado	529	1,630,180	232	143,801
Connecticut	783	3,884,353	341	598,826
Delaware	223	721,092	136	87,531
District of Columbia	177	838,357	95	83,900
Florida	4,090	20,245,897	1,871	2,635,096
Georgia	900	4,077,616	322	405,561
Hawaii	164	677,400	64	61,901
Idaho	109	523,850	40	50,694
Illinois	1,957	8,149,220	999	946,912
Indiana	650	2,831,953	311	317,585
Iowa	474	1,425,778	184	158,665
Kansas	460	1,363,923	178	103,960
Kentucky	329	1,130,537	142	146,137
Louisiana	347	2,018,730	151	147,549
Maine	168	659,868	75	91,739
Maryland	1,065	4,307,335	550	482,638
Massachusetts	1,351	5,074,541	687	604,858
Michigan	951	8,439,720	380	1,217,440
Minnesota	575	2,875,632	203	489,367
Mississippi	188	803,735	97	126,962
Missouri	809	3,273,612	379	431,486
Montana	142	387,347	59	20,450
Nebraska	292	3,864,505	153	238,470
Nevada	300	1,523,564	164	211,414

State of Residence	Gross estate, tax purposes [1]		Net estate tax	
	Number	Amount	Number	Amount
New Hampshire	207	682,735	102	94,771
New Jersey	1,528	5,845,773	719	583,693
New Mexico	200	581,845	96	68,503
New York	3,156	17,657,621	1,539	2,425,496
North Carolina	970	3,709,205	430	409,190
North Dakota	45	233,142	* 18	* 12,693
Ohio	1,360	5,276,026	552	457,293
Oklahoma	320	1,146,682	173	147,687
Oregon	306	1,271,623	156	117,853
Pennsylvania	1,497	6,044,429	641	618,191
Rhode Island	197	675,120	69	69,145
South Carolina	285	1,429,461	131	126,410
South Dakota	113	559,505	* 21	* 8,229
Tennessee	519	1,907,851	228	206,705
Texas	1,708	7,601,993	833	1,021,141
Utah	136	582,465	43	68,946
Vermont	94	606,845	33	87,589
Virginia	1,149	4,106,031	507	470,479
Washington	720	2,527,374	294	275,636
West Virginia	171	485,637	106	53,936
Wisconsin	592	2,332,999	309	248,192
Wyoming	62	220,794	41	23,807
Other areas [2]	81	434,037	58	64,917

NOTE: Detail may not add to total because of rounding.

* *Estimates should be used with caution because of the small number of sample returns on which they are based.*

[1] Gross estate is shown as the value used to determine estate tax liability. The value could be determined as of the decedent's date of death or six months thereafter (i.e., alternate valuation method).

[2] Includes U.S. territories, U.S. citizens domiciled abroad, and a small number of returns for which state of residence was unknown.

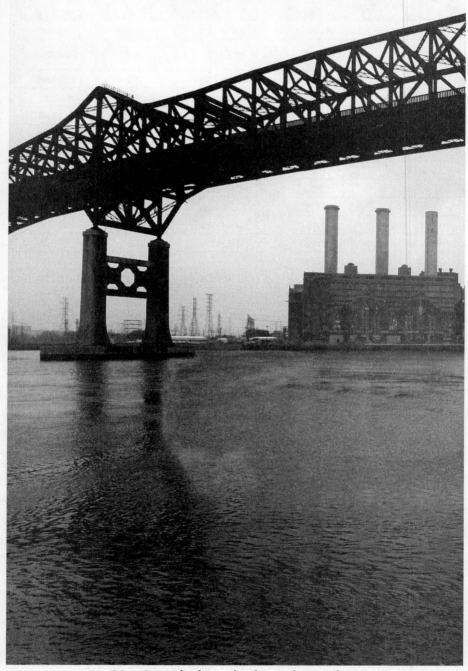

New Jersey highway bridge and waterfront

CHAPTER 5

Wills

The typical picture of reading a will involves a family, dressed head to toe in black, sitting around Grandpa's book-lined study, fidgeting while an elderly lawyer sitting behind the leather-topped desk cleans his glasses and clears his throat before rasping, "Being of sound mind and body … ." The scene is pure Hollywood, and most lawyers will tell you to save the drama for personal letters and keep your will legally correct and clearly stated to avoid potential problems. Make sure beneficiaries know what they are getting so that the day after the funeral, your family can be at home and not in a lawyer's office getting tied up in more drama. Death brings out many characteristics and emotions ranging from numbness to anger to shock, none of which include clear thinking. Determining who is getting which possessions left by the decedent can erupt into bitter arguments. The one person in the best position to resolve the dispute is the one whose voice is gone. Unless he or she has irrevocably disposed of property before dying, the deceased speaks through his or her will.

A will is a legal document in which you identify what people or institutions receive money and property from your estate after your death. It also serves to appoint — or request — guardianship of children or adults who are your legal responsibility and designates, as well as an executor to manage your estate after you die. With standard will forms available on the Internet and in office supply stores, it might seem that preparing a will is easy. But choosing the wrong kind of will, one that does not conform to the laws of your state, such as not having proper witnesses, leaving out key language required by law, or having inadequate particulars, can mean that state law — as applied by the court — will decide what happens to your estate.

There are legal devices called will substitutes, such as a living trust, that can accomplish many of the things a will is designed to do, but it is still a good idea to have a will in addition to your other estate-planning options. The will should round out the estate plan and close any inadvertent loopholes. This is because the state imposes its will on the estate if you do not write one of your own. If you die leaving possessions behind, someone has to divvy them up — and the state assumes that responsibility if you do not do a good job of it.

When you die with a valid will in place, you die "testate." If you do not have a will when you die, then you died "intestate," and then laws in New Jersey determine what happens to your belongings. Because your debts also have to be paid after you die, including federal and state taxes, these creditors will be paid first, and then your beneficiaries will get what is left over.

Most experts will tell you that, for the relatively low cost of having a will prepared by a lawyer, the safety and protection it provides is worth the investment of time and money to get it right. However, before you can ask about a will, you should know what goes into one.

Will Basics

To make sure your will is legal and can be executed, some essential information is necessary. Using your legal name in your will — the one that is on your birth certificate and under which you file tax returns — makes it harder for someone to challenge your will, whether this is the state, a person, or an institution.

As you are a resident, New Jersey will have jurisdiction over your will. That means after you die your will is submitted to probate court. The address listed in your will should be the state in which you vote, hold a driver's license, and have your primary residence. Documentation is necessary to prove the state in which you live.

Another important point about where you live is whether your state has a community property law on the books. If so, then whatever property falls into your state's definition of community property will be jointly owned by a wife and a husband, potentially limiting what you can do with that property in your will. New Jersey is not a community property state.

One more state-related issue is ownership of property outside New Jersey. If you live in New Jersey but own a condo in another state, the out-of-state property will not be handled by the New Jersey court directly. The state agency or court in the state where the property is located will oversee the transition of ownership. When preparing your will, you need to take this into account. Just because you own property does not mean you get to control what happens to it after your death.

Wills Defined

The will that most people think of, called a simple will, is a legal document that applies to only one person. But to be legal, all wills need to include a number of elements. The will needs to identify who you are, your beneficiaries, your executor, the directions you leave for the care of people for whom you are responsible, and the distribution of your assets.

These are basic elements every will needs to have:

- **Beneficiary:** The individual(s) or group(s) that will receive the property.

- **Executor:** Also called a personal representative, this is the individual who handles the property you are leaving behind. If you die without a will, the court appoints an administrator, frequently a spouse or adult child, who will serve in the same capacity of handling all the paperwork, preparing of assets, dealing with likely heirs, handling claims from creditors, making payments on outstanding debt, and other estate-related matters.

- **Clauses:** The sections in your will that likely organize the information in a specific order.

  o **Opening clauses:** Lay out the basic information about who you are and set the stage for the clauses that follow:

    ▶ *Introductory clause identifies you as the person who is making the will.*

    ▶ *Family-statement clause introduces and identifies the family members who will be referred to later in the will.*

    ▶ *Tax clause explains how the taxes of your estate will be paid.*

  o **Survival clause:** This clause leaves everything in your estate to one named person. Married people frequently do this to ensure that everything goes to the surviving spouse.

  o **Guardianship clause:** The appointment of a guardian for minor children (under the age of 18); a successor guardian should also be named as a backup.

  o **Giving clauses:** These clauses leave specific bequests, or property that is identified by name and description, to beneficiaries and explain what property goes to which person and under what circumstances. These can be as broad or explicit as you want. They are divided according to the following categories:

▶ ***Real property clauses:*** *Statements that match property with a person. For example: You want your spouse, Susan, to have the house, and your brother, Fred, to have your antique baseball-card collection.*

▶ ***Personal property clauses:*** *Used when you want to be explicit in your instructions. For example: You want Teddy to get the Google stock, and Elizabeth gets the General Motors stock.*

o **Residuary clause, or residue:** Addresses the "leftovers," the balance of your estate that you do not single out in detail in a specific clause. The residuary clause is essential for any kind of will to make sure that anything you forget or might have acquired after the will was prepared can be distributed. Naming at least one beneficiary is a good idea to keep your assets out of the hands of the courts; naming two or more alternative beneficiaries is better. For example: You want Bertha Jones, your second cousin twice removed, and her husband, Bubba Jones, to benefit from what is not given to anyone else. If either or both of them predeceases you, then all of the balance of your estate goes to Bubba Jones, Jr.

o **Appointment clause:** Identifies the person who will manage your estate. For example: Robert Anthony, your best friend since college, will serve as the executor of your estate.

o **Fiduciary powers clause:** The language that gives your executor the power to serve as your executor, including any duties that go beyond the basic requirements in New Jersey. For example: Robert Anthony will have the ability to provide your spouse, children, and parents with income until your estate is settled.

o **Ending clauses:** These include the legalities to meet statutory requirements so that your will is legal and valid, which include (but are not limited to) your signature, date and location of the signing, and witnesses.

Your will can be as broad or specific as you choose. As one piece of your overall estate plan, your will should be seen as one of several tools and prepared accordingly.

If you want to keep your affairs private, then a more broad will would be in order. Once a will is entered in New Jersey surrogate court, anyone can read it because it becomes a public record. If you have seen the children of a deceased friend get into fistfights over a raggedy old couch or go to court over an off-shore investment account, you might want to go into more detail.

There are different kinds of wills from which to choose to meet your specific needs. The format of these wills changes depending on who is represented in the will, what the will is designed to do, or how it is prepared.

Tips for Creating Your Will

Essentials elements for a valid will include:

- **Being in written form.** Wills that are given verbally might not stand up in court.

- **Your name and age.**

- **"Being of sound mind."** This means you know the property in your possession and the people or institutions identified as beneficiaries.

- **Clear statement and intention to transfer property.**

- **Signed voluntarily.**

- **Witnessed properly.**

- **Executed properly.** The will must include a statement that attests to the fact that this is your will, the date and place it is signed, and that it is signed in front of witnesses.

Mistakes to avoid in your will include:

- Making dramatic personal statements that have nothing to do with the distribution of property, which can end up creating confusion.

- Not being specific enough — if language is ambiguous, it is subject to interpretation, and the court makes the final ruling.

- Not asking someone to be your executor or take power-of-attorney responsibilities.

- "Leftover" and "not enough" property to meet the conditions of your will.

- Using beneficiaries as witnesses who sign the will — you want to avoid the potential appearance of a conflict of interest or having undue influence over the person making the will.

- Making many changes at once or over time and not creating a new will; excessive changes can lead to confusion.

A few more things ...

The original document

If the original will is stored in a safe deposit box, it could become inaccessible after your death if that box only is in your name. Have your lawyer retain the original will so that it is readily accessible.

Other will-related documents

Your original durable power of attorney, medical power of attorney, living will, and any other documents related to incapacitation should also be stored in your lawyer's office. Those taking responsibility for making medical, financial, or other decisions should have a copy of this power of attorney.

Copies

Choosing to keep your will private is a decision you will need to make based on a conversation with your lawyer. Unusual clauses or issues might warrant making copies of the documents and sharing them with key people in advance so that nobody is surprised when the will is executed. Your wishes regarding what should happen if you were to become incapacitated and who is responsible for making decisions on your behalf should be shared with all family members and close friends. This way, there can be no question about what you would like done.

**Note: Do not sign copies of a will, or it might qualify as a legal "duplicate original." Write "COPY" in ink on each page just to make sure nobody can claim a copy is the original.

Especially in the case of serious illness and a do-not-resuscitate (DNR) order, a living will, and organ donation, your physicians and other medical providers need to have copies of your will. Your doctors might have their own form for you to fill out related to these matters; be sure to check.

The "who" of a will

Mutual will: This is a plan for your estate that is prepared in conjunction with another person.

For example, sisters Carol and Angie agree to support their disabled brother, Brian, and Grandma Jane. So, they decide that no matter who dies first, 40 percent of either estate goes to Brian, 40 percent goes to Grandma Jane, and the remaining 20 percent goes to other beneficiaries. When the other person dies, 50 percent of her estate goes to Brian, 20 percent goes to Grandma Jane, and the remaining 30 percent goes to other beneficiaries. If Grandma Jane dies before Carol or Angie, her portion goes to Brian.

Joint will: This is one legal document that is for any two people, such as you and your spouse. The problem with this kind of will is that it is irrevocable, which means it cannot be changed after one of the two parties dies. The reason is that all decisions must be made by both people. A lawyer can tell you when this kind of will is a good idea, but most lawyers suggest separate wills to avoid complications. Joint wills are recognized in New Jersey.

Simple will: A single legal document that is written by one person that identifies who you are, your beneficiaries, your executor, the directions you leave for the care of people for whom you are responsible, and the distribution of your assets.

The "what" of a will

Pourover will: This will place some property into a trust that was established while you were still alive.

Testamentary trust will: This will move your assets into one or more trusts after your death. *See Chapter 6 for more information on trusts.*

The "how" of a will

Holographic will: This is a handwritten document that is signed by you but not witnessed by anyone else. Some states, including New Jersey, recognize a handwritten will as valid. *See Chapter 11 for more information on how this works in New Jersey.*

Nuncupative will: Also called an oral will, this is a spoken will. Some states only allow this kind of will if someone is literally on his or her deathbed, and it only covers personal property of little or no value. New Jersey law does not recognize nuncupative wills.

Video will: Except in Nevada, a will recorded on a videotape or digital video device (DVD) will not be accepted as a legal document. Some states will, in extreme circumstances, allow a will to be recorded by a terminally ill person from a deathbed — literally. Recording messages to loved ones might be something you want to do, but it is better to prepare legal documents, such as a will, with a lawyer.

It is important to consider how the will you prepare will complement or conflict with other elements of your estate plan.

• *Did You Know?* •

"Nontraditional" children are becoming as common as the "traditional" kind — the biological offspring of a heterosexual couple. When parents are not legally married, some biological offspring may be considered illegitimate, but federal and state law typically define children in the traditional sense.

Over time, legally adopted children have become synonymous with biological children in the eyes of the law. But in an era when divorce, infertility, and same-sex couples mean children become part of a family though in vitro fertilization (IVF), adoptions originating in a foreign country, and stepchildren, inheritance can be a tricky thing.

A child born outside a legally recognized union — in most states, this is defined as a marriage between a woman and a man; although, New Jersey recognizes civil unions and domestic partners, though these are not "marriages" — will automatically inherit his or her mother's estate. An inheritance from the biological father is not necessarily automatic.

Many state laws allow a child to inherit from a man who is identified as the father through a paternity test. The father also can marry the mother after the child is born and acknowledge himself as the father of the "out of wedlock" daughter/son. If paternity — the action taken to establish the biological relationship of an adult in a parent-child relationship — is not established, then a child cannot inherit from the estate of the unidentified parent.

☑ Watch Out for This

☐ You must legally adopt stepchildren for them to be considered part of your family; if you do not adopt them, and your will directs your estate to fund trust funds for "my children," only those minors who are recognized by the state — not you — as yours will be able to receive a bequest.

☐ A paternity test is the comparison of blood taken from the potential father against a blood sample of the child.

☐ A paternity suit is a legal action that is initiated to establish a man as the biological father of a child.

☐ While the question of paternity is typically associated with the father, a paternity test can be used to establish the biological relationship of a mother as well, in the case of abandonment or other circumstances in which a mother is not clearly identified.

The "Other" Will

Many people prepare a living will at the time they draw up the will for their estate, even though it has nothing to do with your house, car, or checking account. A living will or medical directive is a document in which you spell out the decisions you have made about your medical care while you are still alive. The idea is to decide what kind of measures you want — or do not want — taken on your behalf if you should become incapacitated.

All states — including New Jersey — now recognize living wills, but the documents are not uniform. Some states will only allow living wills to apply to a person who is permanently unconscious or has a terminal illness. Other states will allow them for advanced-stage illnesses, such as the final stages of Alzheimer's disease, when death is not imminent.

To make sure your wishes are followed, you need to understand what is and is not allowed by New Jersey laws. A statutory living will is one that complies with the statutes, or laws, of your state. *Chapter 11 further discusses statutory living wills.* A nonstatutory living will does not comply with the laws of New Jersey. The differences between a statutory and nonstatutory living will might seem obvious, but like most legalities, the details are critical. A statutory document will likely provide more protection for the physicians and nurses carrying out your wishes.

Wording is also essential. A statement such as "I do not want to become a burden to my family" is vague. Your living will should be specific and address your medical history, so consulting your doctor about what-if scenarios is essential to understanding what kinds of lifesaving measures might be taken to keep you alive. If you have a history of congestive heart failure in your family and have been diagnosed with the same condition, but do not want extraordinary measures — such as being kept alive by feeding tube or respirator — taken to prolong your life, your wish needs to be spelled out.

Another way to make sure your wishes are followed regarding your medical care is to designate a health care power of attorney (HCPA), also known as a medical power of attorney. Your HCPA involves designating a person to make medical decisions for you when you cannot do it for yourself by you signing a legal document known as a power of attorney. Many states have laws that allow family members to make some or all of your health care decisions. These family-consent or health-surrogate laws follow a specific order of kinship for who makes a decision; if you are married, your spouse — not your sister — will be your surrogate. Even though the default position of most physicians is to consult the family, having your wishes spelled out in an HCPA relieves your family of having to deal with that issue.

A durable power of attorney can also be used to give someone else the authority to make medical decisions on your behalf. This kind of power of attorney allows an authorized person to act on behalf of the grantor of that power of attorney.

Making decisions about life-sustaining treatment, artificial nutrition and hydration, and organ donation are the advanced directives most people prepare. A DNR order — do not resuscitate if you appear to have died — is an example of the kind of decision you can make and communicate in your living will. Completing an organ donor card will reinforce your decision to make that gift, if that is important to you.

To avoid confusion or conflict at a later date, make sure your living will is properly executed with witnesses present. Then make sure close family members and friends have copies of the document and understand your wishes. That way, when a medical decision needs to be made, there is not any question about what you would want.

• Did You Know? •

The Health Insurance Portability and Accountability Act (HIPAA) is a federal law passed in 1996 that did more than just create more forms for you to sign at the doctor's office. It protects medical insurance coverage for employees when they change or lose their jobs. It also forced the creation and implementation of national standards for conducting electronic medical-care transactions for providers, medical insurance companies/plans, and employers. But it also put into place privacy protections that prevent caregivers from sharing your personal information with anyone not explicitly authorized by you.

Questions were raised about the access to private information for someone holding a health care/medical power of attorney: Can that person be given confidential medical information by medical staff in order to make informed decisions, as the incapacitated person expected?

The answer is yes. A form explicitly giving your designated person access to your information is not necessary. The U.S. Department of Health and Human Services confirmed that the power of attorney supersedes the HIPAA privacy requirements.

It is still a good idea to make sure all your medical care providers — primary care physician, eye doctor, dentist, and any specialists — have a copy of your health care/medical power of attorney on file. This can help avoid delays in case of an emergency.

People Speaking for You

After you are no longer able to speak for yourself, others will speak on your behalf. Those individuals you choose to act for you have a host of legal and moral issues to manage, so choosing who will represent you is a serious matter. The lawyer preparing your will and the executor of your will are the two people who will have the most immediate and significant impact on what happens after you are gone. To choose the best people for these tasks, it is important to know their responsibilities.

Wills attorney

The lawyer you work with to draw up your will needs to be well-versed in federal law regarding estates, in addition to knowing what New Jersey requires and what makes a will valid/legal. If your estate plan includes several planning professionals, such as a CPA or financial planner, then your lawyer needs to be someone who can work well with others.

The more elusive criteria for choosing your legal representative are those things that give you a sense that you can trust and work with this person. You need to be able to share all the details of your estate and wishes so that he or she will be able to give you the best advice. You also need to be comfortable going back repeatedly to make changes to your will that reflect the changes in your life.

Being able to communicate comfortably and effectively is equally important with the person who will manage your estate.

Executor

After you are gone, you want someone to take care of your estate the way you would. That means finding the right person or company to handle the steps that need to be taken after you die. Regardless of the individual(s) you select, there are things that this person must do:

- Guide your will through the probate process to make sure it is accepted as valid. This also means defending the will against any contest challenges.

- Collect your assets.

- Oversee the transition of gifts made to beneficiaries. This might include a title transfer for a house or making sure a life-insurance policy check is made out in the correct name.

- Review, evaluate, and pay any claims against your estate. These include taxes and outstanding bills that are owed.

- Raise the money to pay claims. This can mean selling assets, such as a house or car.

- Prepare and file an accounting of all financial transactions for the court.

Failure to do any of these steps can have serious consequences for the executor, so it is extremely important that the person who agrees to take on this responsibility knows what is expected.

Because this is such a time-consuming, key responsibility, you do have the option to pay your executor a fee for his or her services. Whether you should do this is a decision to discuss with your lawyer.

Although it is impossible to predict how someone will handle this kind of responsibility, giving careful thought to who will carry out your wishes is important.

Change and Your Will

Simply put, things happen. This is why it is essential to make sure that changes you experience in your life are reflected in your will. After a will is written, it is not etched in stone — it can be revised or even replaced.

To make a change to a specific portion of your will, you create a codicil. This is a separate legal document that adds to your existing will. It is an easy way to make a few simple changes. When you are older, a codicil is an easy way to protect your will from being challenged due to incompetence. If you only change one part, then the codicil might be successfully challenged, but not the majority of your will.

You might wind up changing your will without even realizing it. If you bequest specific property to someone, such as a boat, but then you sell it, or it sinks during a storm, it will be addressed by the court. No matter what the reason, if property is missing from your estate that is named in your will, then it is considered adeemed. Ademption statutes govern the distribution of your belongings, and the state will take over if items are missing. There are ways to avoid this problem, such as having "back-up" property to serve as a substitute.

If a beneficiary in your will dies before you do, this creates an antilapse. If the property exists and no contingent beneficiary is named, then the state steps in if it has an antilapse statute. If your state does not have such a statute, then the property would most likely be covered by the residuary clause, but it is best to check with an attorney to be sure.

Maybe at the time of your death you are carrying a ton of debt that you were going to pay off in the near future. An unexpected departure is something you can plan for in your will, but it takes some planning. The usual method for paying off debt is to sell property in the estate, such as jewelry, antiques, or vacation property. However, if there still is not enough money to take care of those debts, your house might have to be sold, leaving your family homeless. Some states have a homestead exemption statute that protects the family home from being sold. However, it is not a 100-percent guarantee, so work with your estate-planning team to figure out how to address this and other "what-if" scenarios.

CHAPTER 6
Trusts

The image many people have of a child with a trust fund is someone with access to all the money necessary to pay for a college education, an extended tour of Europe, or a carefree future without money problems. The reality is that you do not have to be independently wealthy to set up a trust, and their uses are significantly more diverse than the aforementioned stereotypes.

The basic idea behind a trust is to set aside specific property for specific people or institutions so that you, not the courts, decide what will happen to your estate. Knowing what you want to put into a trust, who benefits from it, and the price to be paid — set-up fees, taxes, time — is essential to making sure you choose the right trust.

There are at least a dozen different kinds of trusts with various combinations of legal and tax implications, so there is no such thing as a "standard" trust. A book like this one can help you learn what a trust is, but any "one-size-fits-all" trust template is a disaster waiting to happen.

Each trust is customized to meet the needs of the individual — that is what makes a trust so attractive and difficult. Laws and tax requirements at the federal and state levels are constantly changing, and so are your needs. With the extremely real possibility that your trust could end up in probate or in the hands of the government, it is essential to work with an estate planner and lawyer to make sure you have the proper documents in place so that your trust is legal and enforceable.

To make sure the outcome you want is the one you get, learn what a trust is, its benefits, and its drawbacks. The steps to set up a trust and the elements of a trust can be easy enough to understand: Identify what property will be included, who benefits, who manages the trust, tax implications for all the people involved, and how the law governs all that activity. The tricky part is learning about the different kinds of trusts and matching them up with your wishes.

What is a Trust?

A trust is a legal arrangement that involves the transfer of property from the original owner to a person or a company for the purpose of holding and maintaining the property until it is handed over to the beneficiary — the individual or institution designated to receive the property.

It seems straightforward enough — until you get into the many legal terms, people, laws, and taxes that go into the creation of a trust. With many interchangeable terms, some of which are as confusing as the Greek or Roman terms from which they originated, a list of who is who and what is what is helpful. The following situation will assist you with recognizing the roles each person plays in a trust.

People: Aunt Tara wants to set up a trust for her house so that her niece Betsy will have a place to set up her veterinary clinic after she finishes her education. However, she does not know when Betsy will graduate, so she wants her grandson Charles to take care of the place if she — Aunt

Tara — dies. In case something happens to Charles, his wife, Kim, will take on that responsibility.

- **Trustor (Aunt Tara):** The person who sets up the trust. Other names commonly used are creator, donor, settlor, or grantor.

- **Beneficiary (Betsy):** The individual(s) or group(s) that will receive the property in the trust. This can be a single person, a group of people, one group, several groups, or a combination of any of these.

- **Trustee (Charles):** The person or company that will oversee or manage the trust after it is established. This person (or group) will make sure the property in the trust is safe and in good order until it is turned over to the beneficiary. This includes paying any taxes, performing repairs, or doing anything else an owner would do. The trustee is obligated to carry out the terms of the trust and can be paid for this effort, if terms for this are included in the trust language.

- **Successor trustee (Kim):** Someone who will step in if the primary trustee is unable to serve or cannot continue to manage your trust. This person will have the same legal obligations for managing the trust as the original trustee, should the successor assume the management responsibilities.

The individual or company designated to serve as trustee carries a significant amount of responsibility and needs to be someone you trust implicitly. The potential for a conflict of interest or being swayed by the temptation to do something inappropriate — such as stealing from the trust or neglecting the work — needs to be considered. Putting language in the trust documents that spells out the responsibilities of the trustees is essential, and creating a mechanism of oversight and removal will also prevent your heirs from losing what is supposed to be theirs.

Things and strings: Aunt Tara's house sits on 4 acres of land with an outbuilding to store the lawn tractor and other equipment. Over the years, she sold the other 12 acres, so she invested the money into a mutual fund. Aunt Tara had her lawyer set up a trust fund that gives Betsy the interest from the mutual fund to pay tuition when it is due in the fall, but Aunt Tara's mutual fund will not go to Betsy until she graduates from college. The house in the care of Charles will also go to Betsy after she graduates.

- **Property:** Anything you want to give to other people, also referred to as principal. There are all kinds of legal terms for the "stuff" you own, and you have to make sure you use the right words to identify everything from money in a safe or checking account to a rocking chair or commemorative baseball. This can be real property or real estate (10-acre farm), tangible personal property (the things you can touch, such as a lawn tractor and other equipment), or intangible personal property (financial assets, such as certificates of deposit).

- **Trust agreement:** The legal document that spells out the terms of a trust, including the people and conditions, and the rules that must be followed. Some are state or federal laws, and others are specific conditions (trust fund).

- **Funding a trust:** The placement of property in a trust; that same property will be called trust principal when it is under the auspices of the trust agreement.

- **Provisions:** The clauses that spell out how you want your wishes carried out. Distribution provisions will identify to whom the income will be given and the frequency of those distributions (pay tuition when it is due in the fall). Special provisions encompass all requirements that are unique to the beneficiary or the assets (graduates from college).

- **Legal title:** This gives the trustee ownership of the property in the trust for the duration of the trustee's responsibility (house in Charles' care).

- **Beneficial title:** Also known as equitable title, this is the right of the person or institution to take possession of or benefit from the property in the trust (goes to Betsy).

The plan can be incredibly clear, but whether the end result matches that plan depends on the kind of trust you choose, the way the documents are worded, and the way the people involved carry out their tasks. It is easier to make mistakes than it is to get it right, and those mistakes can be costly for loved ones. If you are not careful, they can inherit a big mess instead of the things you want them to have.

One way to avoid such a mess is to carefully choose a trustee who will carry out your wishes and do so legally. Being a trustee is more than just whipping out a checkbook and signing a few papers now and then.

Talking to Your Estate Planner About Trusts

Before you sit down with your estate planner, take some time to think about the questions you have regarding your life circumstances. Here are a few to keep in mind:

- What are the tax consequences for this trust? What about capital gains?

- What happens to the "leftovers" in a trust — cash, property, and everything else?

- Will there be a problem if the trust beneficiary dies before you do?

- What happens if the terms of a trust are not met — for example, Bobby quits school before his educational trust is spent?

- When does a specific-use trust terminate — for example, if Aunt Mimi's disability trust is still in place after she dies?

- What happens to an irrevocable trust if the situation changes?

- What are the advantages and disadvantages for a single person in setting up a trust?

- What happens if some of the property in your trust is community property and you divorce?

- If you end up divorced, what happens to the education trust fund that Mom and Dad are funding for little Suzy?

Things to consider ...

An estate planner also can help you address some of the unexpected or unusual life circumstances that might not be on your mind. There are also legal ramifications for your death that might not come up during your life. For example, unmarried partners do not get the same automatic consideration that a legally married couple has. A qualified terminable interest property trust (QTIP) is not an option for a couple that does not have a legally documented marriage.

Some other things that affect the legality and terms of a trust include:

- Foreign-born spouse

- Nonbiological "family" members

- Same-sex couples

- Living together — as opposed to a formal or common-law marriage

- Adoption

- Pets

- Divorce

- Multiple marriages — offspring and spouses

- Incapacitation

- Medical condition / serious illness

- Permanent disability

- Natural disaster affecting property

- Stock / real-estate market crash

Types of Trusts

A trust can be set up to take effect while you are alive (inter vivos), or it can take effect after you die (testamentary). Some can be changed (revocable), and some cannot be changed no matter what (irrevocable). Some trusts can be terminated or ended, while others cannot. The purpose of a trust can result in a tax exemption or a higher tax rate, depending on what the current tax law allows.

There are trusts for yourself and trusts for other people, and many of the reasons for setting up either kind are the same — getting tax benefits, staying out of probate court, protecting assets from creditors, or making sure money is available "just in case" for matters like education, severe illness, or a disability. Considering all life's possibilities to decide which trust(s) would be helpful is a daunting task. Another way to look at the situation is to consider the kinds of trusts that already exist and have defined legal and tax consequences.

Trusts fall into a number of categories that can be described by different criteria. One criterion is the beneficiary. A marital-dedicational trust is specific to the surviving, legal spouse of the deceased. A bypass trust will transfer property to someone other than your spouse, such as a child or grandchild, but allow him or her to still benefit from the property in the trust. Some states even allow you to create a trust for your pets.

Another criterion is the reason for the trust. If you want to protect the beneficiary's property so that it is available for a specific reason when it is needed, you would use a protective trust. A discretionary trust gives the trustee the ability to distribute income and property to a variety of beneficiaries; he or she also has the option to control the distributions to a single beneficiary as he or she decides is appropriate. This offers some flexibility, as does a dynasty trust; also known as a wealth trust, it can last for several generations, or be set up to never end. This kind of trust helps people with a vast amount of wealth control the distribution of that money and property over a long period of time. However, many states limit noncharitable trusts to 90 years.

The overarching requirements of a trust create yet another group. A split-interest means more than one individual benefits from the trust: One person or charity would have an interest in the trust for a specific period of time, and then another person or charity receives the property that remains. A support trust requires a trustee to pay only the income and property necessary to cover the cost of education or assistance, such as health care or nursing home fees, of the beneficiaries.

Some trusts are automatically irrevocable, so you have to make sure you know what you are signing before you pick up the pen. However, many trusts can be set up as revocable or irrevocable, with a variety of conditions that put the trust into one of the categories already defined by tax law. These laws continue to change to keep up with creative efforts to avoid taxes.

These conditions and restrictions make it important to consult an estate-planning specialist to discuss the trust options that will help you achieve your goals and understand the tax implications of your choices.

Following is a list of the different types of trusts:

- **Burial trust:** Provides the funds necessary to cover the cost of burial or cremation arrangements. This can be a revocable trust, but after your death, it becomes irrevocable, and the trust cannot be used for anything else.

- **Charitable trust:** Offers the benefits of tax-free gifts for the donor. A charitable remainder trust gives gifts of interest income that are paid to specific beneficiaries, such as your spouse, for a specific period of time; at the end of that time period, a charity receives whatever is left in the trust. A charitable lead trust, or a front trust, gives the charity a specific gift before all other beneficiaries receive anything. Both are split-interest trusts. Split-interest trusts make distributions to both charitable and noncharitable beneficiaries, while providing tax benefits to their donor.

- **Crummey trust:** An exceedingly complicated trust normally set up in conjunction with an irrevocable life insurance trust to make the payments for a life insurance policy. This is the kind of trust that requires an estate-planning attorney.

- **Educational trust:** This is a kind of protective trust that sets aside money specifically for education-related expenses, such as tuition, training fees, books, or supplies. These trusts regularly include provisions to stop payments if the student drops out of school or flunks many classes.

- **Generation-skipping transfer trust (GSTT):** A tax-saving trust designed to benefit multiple generations after you are gone.

- **Grantor-retained trusts:** These are irrevocable and non-charitable, which means they cannot be changed and the beneficiary is not a charity. There are three common types: A grantor-retained annuity trust (GRAT) gives a fixed amount of money at predetermined times, often at regularly scheduled intervals; a grantor-retained unit trust (GRUT) pays a specific percentage to the beneficiary; and a grantor-retained incomes trust (GRIT) designates specific people to receive certain property, such as stocks or a house, but the income or use of the property stays with you until your death.

- **Living trust:** Created while you are still alive, this trust allows you to be the grantor, trustee, and beneficiary, if you choose.

- **Marital dedication trust:** Puts property into a trust that is exclusively for your spouse, who decides what happens to the property after your death.

- **Minor trust:** A way to give gifts to minors that avoids the gift tax and keeps the property safe until the minor becomes an adult and can take ownership of the trust.

- **Qualified terminable interest property trust (QTIP):** This trust is a marital deduction trust. But instead of your spouse deciding who gets the property after your death, the grantor makes that decision.

- **Spendthrift trust:** A trust set up for someone who will be unable to handle their own affairs, for example, someone who is mentally incompetent or might have financial problems and needs protection from creditors. The beneficiary does not own the property in the trust, just the payments that are made from the trust.

- **Special needs trust:** A support trust for a disabled person under the age of 65 (you or anyone else), this trust makes payments on the beneficiary's behalf, as required by the state as reimbursement. After the beneficiary dies, the property in the trust is paid to other beneficiaries. This trust is designed to protect your property from seizure by the government or a creditor seeking reimbursement.

- **Supplemental needs trust:** A support trust designed to provide income to a handicapped, elderly, or disabled person to supplement this person's income, but is structured in a way that does not reduce or jeopardize the eligibility of that person to receive public or private benefits. This trust is designed to protect your property from seizure by the government or a creditor seeking reimbursement.

- **Testamentary trust:** Created by the terms of your will after your death.

- **Totten trust:** This is a bank account that, upon your death, immediately passes to the named beneficiary.

There are also special trusts for specific things, such as real estate, life insurance, or pension benefits. Choosing which trust will meet your needs and those of your estate is a difficult process. This information is a way for you to familiarize yourself with the choices, but an estate-planning specialist is the best person to help you decide whether you need a trust and which one will be the best choice.

• *Did You Know?* •

If you have a modest estate, but you still want your minor children to inherit your property, you can use the Uniform Transfer for Minors Act (UTMA) or the Uniform Gift to Minors Act (UGMA). Most states, including New Jersey, have adopted this legislation, which allows you to create a custodial account for a minor.

A custodial account, which can be in the form of a trust, allows you to deposit money or property in an account set up by a bank or a brokerage firm. You name yourself as the custodian — trustee — of the account while you are alive and name a successor to take over those responsibilities after you die. This new custodian will serve in that capacity until the child reaches 18, 21, or 25, depending on the state law.

☑ Watch Out for This

☐ Some states hand over the ownership of the account to the child when he or she turns 18, and you have no say after that.

☐ Accounts for children over the age of 13 are subject to federal income tax at the children's rate. This will most certainly be lower than your tax rate, but the implications of this need to be considered.

☐ If you create an UGMA or UTMA account, this can reduce the amount of court paperwork and supervision, thereby lowering estate costs.

☐ Even if you create this kind of account, you must still name a legal guardian for your children in your will. The legal guardian can also be custodian of this kind of account, but naming a custodian of an account is not the same as naming a legal guardian.

Pros and Cons of Forming a Trust

Trusts provide some excellent benefits, but they are not the perfect solution for everything. One benefit is that some trusts can reduce the amount of taxes that have to be paid before and after you die. But if your trust is set up improperly, it might have to pay income tax. A trust can protect your assets from your creditors or those of your beneficiaries, but only if it is set up properly.

More private than a will, which becomes public record upon your death and makes the details of your estate available to anyone who wants access, a trust can keep others out of your personal business. In many cases, a trust can help keep your estate out of probate court, and it is more difficult to contest a trust than a will. The flexibility of a trust allows you to make changes and can even help with financial issues if you become disabled during your life.

The downside is that it costs money to set up a trust, and numerous scams are out there, foreign and domestic. So, if you are not careful, you could lose the property you want to go to your loved ones and favorite charity. There also is the possibility that your trustee will abscond with the contents of the trusts and head for a nonextradition country. Whether trusts are worth all the hassle and potential risk is up to you — and that is why is it essential to work with estate-planning specialists when setting up trust(s).

Do's and Don'ts for Trusts

The following tips are things to consider when you are preparing your trust:

- Think of choosing a trust as a dry run for your estate planning. Consider all possible life scenarios and how a trust will or will not help those situations.

- When setting up a trust or trusts, do them all at once so that you can save a few dollars — with any luck — and make sure none of them conflict with the others.

- Put all trust agreements in writing.

- Make sure the proper legal language is used in every agreement.

- Clearly define the trustee responsibilities and obligations. A "passive" trust, which does not define these things, might not be recognized by a court as a trust.

- Clearly identify beneficiaries.

- Clearly define the property in the trust. "Everything in the dining room" is an example of what not to do.

- Make sure the property you put into a trust will meet the needs you identify. Setting aside $100,000 to pay for a college education in the year 2100 might not be enough.

- Carefully choose a trustee who will execute your wishes and take care of all legal obligations.

- Keep an eye on the content and value of each trust over time — fluctuating market conditions and changes in your life might leave a trust underfunded or make it obsolete.

Notes about other information you want to learn:

_____
_____
_____
_____
_____

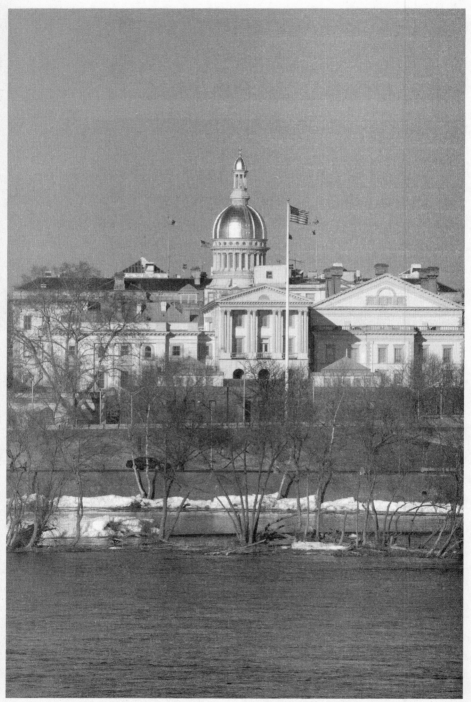

New Jersey state house and capitol complex in Trenton

CHAPTER 7

Insurance

Insurance is one part of your estate plan, and it can be an especially effective part if you have good information and advice tailored to your needs, not those of the person pushing papers across the desk for you to sign. How you want to make that money work for you should guide your shopping and decision-making. Consider:

- **Funeral expenses:** On average, these range from $5,000 - $8,000 but can go much higher.

- **Grief money:** Supports your family during their grieving period so that they do not have to rush back to work to cover bills.

- **Debts:** Cover the cost of money you owe to others so that it does not reduce the size of your estate.

- **Estate costs:** Ready cash to cover estate taxes and costs for distributing your estate and to provide a stipend for your executor.

- **Lost income:** Gives your family access to some of the income you would have earned.

- **Education funds:** Money for school, now or in the future.

- **Funding a trust:** This will add to the property in the trust and be distributed like all other assets in that trust.

- **Taxes:** Giving money to your "probate estate" is a way to make sure your estate has enough money to cover tax payment to state and federal tax collectors.

For a rather small investment, you can provide your beneficiaries with a substantial amount of money, if you choose carefully.

After you die, the insurance company that holds your life insurance policy cuts a check to your spouse, children, or parents, but there is much more to know, including the following:

- Death benefits can be taxed.

- If the beneficiary of your policy dies before you do, the money goes into probate.

- An insurance policy that invests in the stock market might actually lose value, leaving your beneficiaries with less money.

- A serious illness can devastate the assets of your estate, which means the life insurance you wanted to support your family could instead end up in the hands of creditors.

Insurance, like most things in life, is not quite as simple as it once was — or as sales reps like to make it appear. The kind of insurance you have when you are alive can affect your estate as much as the insurance you have for after your death, so this is where the here-and-now affects the future.

Insurance, simply defined, is a method to protect the things we value most. Some insurance is mandated by law (automobile insurance), while some is considered essential (health insurance, although this is also becoming mandated by law), and other kinds are considered a luxury (disability and long-term care). What kind and how much insurance any individual needs is based upon individual circumstances. If you do not own a $20 million country estate, it is unlikely you will need the kind of liability insurance that would protect you against a lawsuit brought by someone who stayed for the weekend and was hurt while riding a horse from your stable.

As part of your overall estate plan, insurance can accomplish some of the more conventional goals people have, such as providing cash to pay taxes so that your family does not have to sell property to settle up with Uncle Sam. What is slightly more uncommon is considering the impact a permanent disability can have on the assets of your estate and how you will maintain that estate until it is passed on to someone else.

Thinking about insurance before you need it is the best way to consider the host of options and tangle of details and conditions related to each option. This requires much "what if" speculation on your part, but educated guesses are possible when you make time to let your imagination run free.

Insurance for Here and Now

Most insurance commercials focus on the worst-case scenario to scare you into buying peace of mind. Though horrible, these situations are exactly what you need to consider. While not fun, considering the effects of a serious illness, debilitating accident, or natural disaster can point you in the right directions for figuring out your insurance needs.

Medical insurance

Frequently referred to as health insurance by those who sell it, the insurance that covers medical costs is almost never used when you are healthy — but you always have to whip out that benefits card when you fill a prescription for strep throat, have a heart attack, or break a bone.

The first question you need to consider is whether your insurance policy will cover your bills when you truly need it to, because if your insurance does not pay, you will have to. That payment can be high enough to wipe out your savings, not to mention any other assets you have built up over time. What most people consider is the amount that is deducted from every paycheck week after week, not the tens of thousands of dollars a hospital will try to collect from you after you have hit your "maximum lifetime benefit."

Even if your family has no history of colon cancer, breast cancer, heart attack, or even high cholesterol, you can still be involved in a workplace accident or a horrible car crash that is not your fault, or contract a rare virus on the only trip you ever take out of the country. Anyone who has children or knows someone who has children knows that trips to the emergency room and doctor's office are the rule, not the exception.

A simple cold going around school can land your child in an intensive care unit (ICU) with walking pneumonia — will your insurance cover a stay in a pediatric ICU? What if your child requires hospitalization while he or she is out of state visiting relatives? Knowing the terms of your medical insurance coverage, beyond the monthly premium, is an essential part of your estate planning. A few simple things to check are:

- What is the maximum lifetime benefit per person? Per policy?

- What serious illnesses are not covered?

- How is a "pre-existing condition" defined, and can that be excluded from your coverage?

- Do you have "out-of-network" coverage? Can you purchase additional coverage if you are going to travel out of your network area? Out of the country?

- What about medical care provided outside the United States — can you get reimbursed for these costs?

- When can you make changes to your coverage?

After you find the answers to these questions, compare the information against your family medical history — do any of the "not covered" illnesses run in your family? Also, consider what is on the horizon for your family, such as a child studying abroad for a year or an overweight spouse starting a new exercise program without consulting a doctor. Paying a slightly higher premium now for better coverage can prevent some devastating bills later.

A person diagnosed with cancer typically does not begin thinking about funding a family trip to Bermuda; that person is thinking about extensive treatments, not being able to coach Little League, and maybe being unable to work for an extended period of time. Do not leave everything in the hands of your insurance agent. Preparing for these "what-if" situations is your job.

Disability insurance

A disability insurance policy will make payments to you to cover living expenses and replace your lost income as a result of your inability to hold a job. So, if you cannot work because you are sick, get hurt, or for some other reason, this insurance will replace some of your lost income. Imagine what could happen to your savings if you are stuck at home in bed, but the mortgage payment, utilities bills, and furnace repair invoices keep coming.

Your ability to leave anything for your loved ones after you are gone is largely dependent upon the work you do while you are alive. Though disability insurance will not replace 100 percent of your income, it would certainly be better than nothing. The question is whether the conditions and restrictions make it a worthwhile investment. If you feel it is a good idea, determine what kind of disability insurance will meet your needs.

Many different disability plans are out there, but they fall into two types: short- or long-term. Short-term disability provides benefits for about three months; some plans go a little longer, but they are a temporary fix. Long-term disability can provide benefits for years but does eventually end — frequently at 65, when you become eligible for social security. The benefits are as varied as the plans available. Some details to look for include:

- **When the policy goes into effect:** Some policies do not begin to make payments until you have been out of work for a specific period of time; they do not make payments the moment you are disabled.

- **How payments are calculated:** Some policies replace a percentage of your income, on average ranging from 50 – 75 percent.

- **Definition of disability:** You might have to be unable to work at any job, or payments might be made if you are unable to work in your chosen profession.

- **Premium payments:** How they are calculated can depend on the percentage of income replaced — more money means a higher premium — or some other criterion.

The federal government also provides a social security disability benefit for which you might be eligible. However, if you think getting only 50 percent of your income reimbursed is not enough, do not count on the government to offer a 100-percent replacement.

While short-term disability can help you through a rough time, long-term disability will have a direct impact on your estate plan. A serious injury not only has the potential to rack up major medical bills not covered by health insurance, but it also can eliminate the possibility of future investments and jeopardize your ability to pay life insurance and other premiums.

Long-term care insurance

The difference between long-term disability and long-term care insurance is that the latter provides payments to cover the cost of medical care. In-home nursing or nursing home fees are examples of what might be covered. While this might bring to mind 89-year-old Aunt Mary who could fall and break her hip, this coverage is for any debilitating injury suffered by anyone at any age.

If you fall at work and injure your back badly enough that you require surgery and months of physical therapy so that you can walk again, your medical insurance might not be enough to cover the entire cost. Again, it is important to understand what the policy will and will not cover and when the payments will begin. If you max out your medical insurance, but your long-term care insurance does not kick in for a year, if ever, the assets in your estate could be in jeopardy.

Looking into all these details before you need to use your insurance is the best way to learn what you need to know. Do not leave it to your family to sort out.

Homeowner's/renter's insurance

If your house is your biggest asset, then protecting it is a no-brainer. The list of possible disasters can keep homeowners up all night immediately before and after buying a house. There is nothing like a down payment and an hour's worth of signing papers to make you realize what is on the line if something goes wrong. Banks are not in the habit of saying, "Your house burned down? Well, then, let's just tear up those loan papers."

Even if you do not own a home, that lease you signed is a legally binding agreement. If you are robbed or the pipes in the apartment above add a waterfall feature to your living room, you are still going to have to pay your rent, and the antique books you wanted to give to niece Amy will not be worth the paper composing the pulp they will resemble.

Making sure you can recoup the loss of your property — both real estate and the things you have to move in boxes — is essential if your estate is to have any value after a disaster, natural or otherwise. Fire, flood, earthquake, tornadoes, snow caving in a roof, wind damage, or anything else you can think of that might possibly damage your home and its contents are the factors to consider when purchasing insurance.

Some homeowners' policies that will pay off the balance of a home mortgage, leaving the bulk of your estate to replace your income if you do not want your family to worry about money after you are gone. Before signing on that dotted line, find out the circumstances under which the policy might not pay off the mortgage. Just because you die does not mean it will pay up.

Automobile insurance

An antique or exotic car collection would warrant an automobile insurance policy with special coverage for the replacement of such a rare vehicle, as opposed to what the average driver needs. That kind of insurance is important to have if your car collection does not fit on a shelf in the family room, but for everyday driving, there are some basic minimums that everyone needs.

If you lease a car, then you know that the leasing agency requires specific limits for personal injury and liability. New Jersey also requires a minimum amount of insurance coverage to legally drive your car — if you have no insurance, you can have your driver's license suspended or revoked. None of this is likely to be a surprise; what might become a surprise is what happens if you are sued or agree to a settlement that results from an automobile accident and you do not have insurance.

If you have teenagers starting to drive, you know your premiums are going to go up. Car rental agencies figured out the risk of young drivers a long time ago; you have to be 25 to sign a car rental agreement, which is a point not to forget when you have to add another driver to your policy. Remember to check into the per-accident and per-person payout amounts as well — they make a difference.

Car insurance only pays out as much as the limits in your policy. If you want a cheap premium and do not bother to look at what those payouts are, you could end up having to pay a considerable sum. Getting your hands on hundreds of thousands of dollars is not easy for most people, so part of your estate planning is checking into your automobile coverage and deciding whether it is adequate.

Umbrella liability insurance

This kind of policy provides added protection for your property that goes beyond homeowner's, renter's, automobile, or any other kind of insurance. If the person you rear-end at a red light thinks you have a good amount of money, he might stop by the We-Will-Sue-For-You law firm with dollar signs in his or her eyes. It is not fair that you should have to defend yourself against a frivolous lawsuit, but better that than losing your house or other property because you did not have adequate protection.

When looking into this kind of insurance, it is important to know what is and is not covered. Look for loopholes that will allow the insurance company to wiggle out of paying a claim.

An umbrella policy is not going to be necessary for everyone, but it is often essential to estate planning for people with a high-value estate because they have plenty to lose before they have a chance to pass it on. An insurance agent who tells you anything to the contrary needs to be crossed off your list.

Shopping around for an insurance agent you can trust will take time, but the benefits are valuable. Making sense of all the possible options and understanding the fine print of all those options — not to mention the legalities of making changes and still having your beneficiaries receive what you expect them to— is only going to happen if you do your homework.

Details, Details

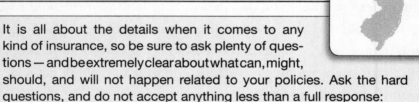

It is all about the details when it comes to any kind of insurance, so be sure to ask plenty of questions — and be extremely clear about what can, might, should, and will not happen related to your policies. Ask the hard questions, and do not accept anything less than a full response:

- Under what circumstances will the benefit not be paid? Find out all degrees of risk, including the worst-case scenario.

- Which of my assets are at risk and from what?

- What kinds of safety nets can insurance provide?

- What kind of insurance does not have a good cost-benefit balance, considering the details of my estate?

- What amount of coverage is excessive for my situation?

- Are there varying degrees of risk among my possible choices? If so, what are they?

- Why would my estate-planning team reject your recommendation?

Policies

With so many options, selecting what you need can be difficult. Check off those you might like to include in your estate plan, and then work with an agent to determine whether you need this kind of coverage.

While you are alive:

_____ Medical

_____ Dental

_____ Vision

_____ Disability — long-term

_____ Disability — short-term

_____ Long-term care

_____ Homeowner's / renter's

_____ Car

_____ Umbrella liability

After death:

_____ Life

_____ Whole life

_____ Universal life

_____ Joint first-to-die or second-to-die

_____ Term life insurance

_____ Annual renewable

_____ Decreasing

_____ Level

_____ Group

_____ Funeral / burial

Insurance for After You Are Gone

Some insurance agents will tell you that all you need is plenty of life insurance to make sure your loved ones are taken care of. But insurance is not that simple. As with wills and trusts, there are many variations on this protection theme. Following are different types of life insurance:

- **Whole life:** Sometimes called cash-value life insurance, this is the kind of policy most people know: After being qualified — smoker/non-smoker, desk jockey/bungee jumper, age 25/ age 75 — the insured person pays a monthly premium on a policy that will, upon his or her death, pay a predetermined, fixed amount of money to his or her beneficiaries. A portion of the fixed (it will never go up or down) premium is invested, another portion is placed into an account — like a savings account — and that cash value is accessible to the policy owner. It can be borrowed against as a loan, or the cash can be taken as the proceeds of the policy instead of the death benefit payout.

  o **Universal life:** A kind of whole life policy that guarantees a minimum return, but the value of the policy can go up or down. If the policy makes more money, the return might be high enough to cover your premium payments.

  o **Joint first-to-die or second-to-die:** Just like it sounds, this is a policy held by two people, and the beneficiary is paid after the first person or second person dies. You decide the payout when you set the terms of the policy.

- **Term life insurance:** Carries an annual premium and pays a specified death benefit to the beneficiary, but it does not have a cash value, so you cannot borrow money from it. The only payment made is to the beneficiary. The premium is based on the amount of insurance you purchase — what will be paid out after your death — and how old you are: Younger people pay less and, as they get older, their premiums rise accordingly. If you stop paying premiums, the death benefit is not paid. A number of different kinds of term policies available:

o **Annual renewable:** A policy that has an annual premium and can be renewed from year to year. Be sure you understand the renewal rights before signing.

o **Decreasing:** Premiums remain the same, but the benefit decreases over time. For example, if you purchase this kind of insurance to pay off your debts after you die — also known as mortgage or credit term insurance — the mortgage you want to insure is $250,000 at the time you purchase the insurance, but the mortgage value when you die is $150,000; the policy pays $150,000. This kind of insurance is recommended only for those who cannot get any other kind of insurance.

o **Level:** Coverage is guaranteed for a specific period of time, or term, such as five, ten, or 20 years at a specific premium. The premium will remain for the five-year period, but at year six, it will go up and remain at that rate through the tenth year, continuing in that direction.

o **Group:** Employers frequently purchase a term life policy for each employee as an added benefit. Employees get an exceptionally low rate, and there is no income tax on the premiums for the first $50,000 of coverage.

• *Did You Know?* •

In order to receive the death benefit from a life insurance policy, a death certificate for the policy holder is required as proof of death.

The most expedient way for your executor to obtain a copy is through the mortuary or other institution that is responsible for handling the body of the deceased. Copies can also be obtained from the county health department.

☑ Watch Out for This

☐ Authorized copies of a death certificate are needed to provide proof of death. As with a birth certificate, you cannot just reproduce a few dozen at your local copy center.

☐ Obtain several copies of the death certificate. Most institutions that require a certificate for proof will retain it for their files.

☐ Money will change hands, so call the county health department to find out the current fee.

Varying Beneficiaries

No matter what kind of insurance you decide to purchase, you can choose different beneficiaries depending on what the policy will do. To start, consider the goal of the policy, per the opening section of this chapter, and who will need or use that money for that purpose. A life insurance policy that is specifically set up to give your family time to grieve might name your spouse as the beneficiary because he or she, not your estate, will pay the utility bills and buy the groceries.

Regardless of whom you name as the beneficiary, it is important to name an alternative beneficiary. If the first beneficiary dies before you or declines the gift, the second person or institution named will receive the benefit.

If the death benefit goes unclaimed, then it is added to your estate and heads to probate for distribution by the court. Creditors and others may get more of the money than family, friends, or a charity you wish to support depending on what is owed at the time of your death.

CASE STUDY: INSURANCE: MORE THAN LIFE COVERAGE

Linda Horn
Chief Executive Officer
Capital Concepts
linda@capitalconcepts.net
www.capitalconcepts.net

Some people only buy insurance, and others diversify their investments. What is the benefit of having a large amount of insurance?

Tax-free income to your family or a charity is a benefit. Proceeds from a policy are often used to provide additional funds to pay estate taxes. Should you own a business or farm, insurance becomes critical to paying federal and state estate taxes, due within nine months of your death. Or perhaps you wish to leave a legacy for future generations or name a charity to continue your legacy.

What are the drawbacks of a large amount of insurance?

The premium payment should never create a financial hardship. After all, life is about living.

Under what circumstance might an insurance company not pay out a death benefit on various types of insurance? (e.g., whole life, term life, accidental death)

During the first two years from the issue date, the policy can be contested for suicides or false statements on the application about known medical history that can be attributed to your death. After two years, or if the above does not apply, all claims are paid.

How is disability insurance a valuable part of estate planning?

Disability is often overlooked, when in fact you have six times the probability of becoming disabled while on the job than of dying on the job. Your largest asset is your income. Protecting your income far exceeds your home, yet we would never consider having no homeowner's coverage.

What other types of insurance, beyond life, are important to an estate plan?

Long-term care insurance is an essential part of your plan. Should you need long-term care, such as in a nursing home or assisted-living facility, your assets will quickly be diminished, and little will be left for your spouse or children. Waiting until you know you need it is like insuring your home when it is on fire; you cannot get it, and if you could, it would be expensive.

What are the benefits of working with an insurance professional?

If you are doing or have done your job of saving properly, a full-time professional is as necessary as the family doctor. A financial advisor works full-time for many years to gain the expertise to get you to your final destination with as few bumps in the road as possible. Approximately 95 percent of do-it-yourselfers lose money, while the use of a professional is just the reverse. The discipline of a balanced approach to risk management and investment will pay off. A good advisor will make you far more money than you ever pay them. Their access to information alone is worth the investment. You do not drill your own teeth or cut your own hair, so why on earth would you invest your life savings with an amateur?

How does a person go about choosing an insurance professional? What characteristics or experience should a potential client look for?

First, ask trusted friends for their recommendations. Second, ask the advisor about their training, years of experience, education, and designations. What is their investment track record and philosophy? Do they share your values and understand you and your goals? Ask for a list of clients you can speak with. And, last, go with your gut.

CHAPTER 8
Retirement Accounts

The "golden years" is public relations speak for that time in life when hair turns white or gray, you do not have to set your alarm clock to get up in the morning, and you choose to have some fun.

People who have access to some kind of pension plan or retirement fund can enjoy traveling or taking the grandchildren out for ice cream and returning them all sugared-up to their parents before heading home. Some who might have done a little saving for retirement and reach the age of 65 — or 67, if you were born after 1960 — can consider their social security income as extra money, not essential for day-to-day living expenses. The group nobody wants to be in is the one that has little or nothing set aside for retirement, because the monthly payment from social security — $1,000 - $2,500 — almost certainly is not going to be enough to live on.

Every one of these scenarios, and a range of others you can imagine, all have implications for your estate planning. Most retirement planning sets a target for how much money you think you will need when you retire so that you can finally stop working. However, that plan is an estimate, and things can happen that mean you have additional money or less money than is needed. This means you will have additional or fewer properties in your estate when you die.

The cost of living can be higher than you anticipated. Maybe you end up with the guardianship of your grandchildren at the age of 70, or the trip to Mongolia was an absolute blast, but you ended with a broken leg when you fell off a camel, and you now have physical therapy bills piling up.

Your Nest Egg

The money you set aside for retirement is yours to keep or lose, depending on the kinds of investment strategies you follow. Looking at the retirement savings plans you have is part of the estate inventory. *Chapter 10 covers these items in more detail.* However, some basic knowledge about what retirement resources people often have is a good place to begin. You might decide you need to make some changes or want to add a newly available method of saving.

You perhaps have some knowledge of your retirement plan — the human resources department at your company might have mandated a meeting every time a policy change was implemented. But what that means within the context of estate planning is different than the context of deciding how much money to take out of your paycheck every week.

Different companies offer different kinds of retirement plan options, and these have changed dramatically over time. Beyond the ever-shifting laws regarding what gets taxed and what does not, many companies have scaled back their participation in retirement plans. Once offered as a virtually guaranteed benefit, pension plans and contributions to retirement accounts are no longer reliably offered. Like any benefit, it is a perk, not mandatory or guaranteed by law, like being paid for the work you do.

It is important to know the kind of retirement program in which you participate and the obligations — if there are any — of the entity offering that plan. Professional associations and various government agencies also have retirement plans available, but their plans tend to be a little different.

After you know what type of plan you have, then you can see how it fits into your estate plan.

Employer pension plans

There are many variations on this theme, so this list will not be exhaustive. It is a place to learn a few things before you chat with estate-planning professionals. Pension and 401(k) plans are the most common ways employers provide a retirement benefit for their employees.

A pension plan is a program that is set up by an employer, including government agencies, to pay employees benefits upon retirement. Each employee has an individual account, and the employer makes a contribution to each employee's account based on the terms of the plan.

There are two common types of pension plans. One is a defined benefit plan from which the employee will receive a specified amount of money upon retirement; the amount of the disbursement made is based on the number of years of employment. The second is a defined contribution plan, which sets a specific amount — a set percentage of income — the employee will put into the plan and makes payments only for the amount of money an employee has contributed to the plan.

A qualified pension plan means the amount of money that the employer puts into an employee's account is not taxed as income during the fiscal year the contribution is made. This means the income is tax-deferred — the employee pays taxes on this money after it is received in the form of a monthly pension payment.

The following conditions exist:

- **Cost-of-living adjustment:** Some plans will have a variable that will allow for annual increases in the payments made to the employee to help cover the cost of rising prices. Not all plans have this feature.

- **Joint-with-survivor pension:** When an employee dies, his or her benefits will be paid to the employee's spouse for the remainder of the spouse's life. If your spouse waives that right, then the employee's pension payments will be larger — no need to set aside extra money for future payments — and the pension payments end when the employee dies.

- **Survivor benefit:** A portion of the deceased employee's pension paid to the surviving spouse. The amount, frequently a percentage, is set by the terms of the pension plan.

- **Waiver:** A written statement declining the right to receive benefits, signed by a spouse. This waiver must be signed to legally sever the right to claim any benefits. An alternative agreement, such as a prenuptial agreement, will not be enough.

- **Limits:** Some pension plans have maximum annual payouts.

A company can avoid putting cash into a retirement fund through distributing profits or shares of the company's stock. With a profit-sharing plan, employees receive a portion of the profits earned by the company; the plan determines the amount that will be contributed to each employee's account. The funds also can be used to invest in programs for components, such as a disability or medical plan.

Stock bonus plans are established by an employer to give shares of a company's stock to employees. When the employee receives the shares, he or she must pay taxes based on the value of the stock. An ESOP is a kind of stock bonus plan. The employer contributes shares of its stock to a qualified trust, an employees only pays taxes based on distributions he or she receives.

Before an employee can receive any distributions or take full ownership of a pension plan, the employee has to be vested, meaning that he or she meets the predetermined requirements contained within the plan, based on the number of years he or she has worked for the employer.

Many employers set up a scale of ownership based on the number of years served. For example, if you work for the company for two years, you are not vested, but when you reach three years, you become 15 percent vested. That means you can take ownership of 15 percent of the company's contribution to your pension plan, plus whatever funds you have contributed. Over time, the percentage of your ownership increases, and at any point beyond the 0 percent mark you will be able to take your contributions and whatever vested percentage you have achieved.

More common today is the 401(k) plan. The equivalent of this concept for not-for-profit entities is the 403(b) plan. Named after the IRS code number defining this kind of plan, the 401(k) allows contributions to be made automatically by your employer via deductions from your paycheck. The advantage is that the money is taken out before taxes, so the amount you pay in taxes now is reduced. You will still have to pay taxes on that money and the interest it earns when you withdraw money from the account. The employer can make a matching tax-deferred contribution to your account. You can take the plan with you when you leave an employer, but the funds must be invested into another approved retirement plan within 60 days, or there will be taxes to pay. In addition, the percentage of the employer contribution you can take with you will likely depend on the vesting schedule for that plan.

Before talking about how you get all this retirement money, there are a few other retirement options to consider.

IRAs and Then Some

A retirement plan option that some companies use also can be used by individuals. An annuity is an investment you create by contributing a specific amount of money over a predetermined period with a fixed rate of return for a number of years. The money put into an annuity is not tax-deductible, or taken pre-tax from your paycheck, if it is an employer-sponsored plan. A distribution will be made to the annuity beneficiary for a fixed term — a specific number of years. The distributions will begin at a predetermined date — typically the year you retire, so that you will be in a lower income-tax bracket — and the distributions will be subject to income tax. The interest on the annuity is accumulated tax-free but will be taxed upon distribution. Here is an example:

In 2008, Rob purchases an annuity from an insurance company for $60,000. The terms of the agreement stipulate that Rob will fund the annuity with ten annual premium payments of $6,000. For ten years, starting in 2018, Rob will receive $9,000 a year from the annuity. The idea is that in 2018, Rob will retire, and his tax bracket will be lower than when he was working full time. Now he will pay lower taxes on that money.

Those annual payments Rob will receive beginning in 2018 will include the income he earned from the annual premiums he paid, which accumulated tax-free while the annuity was being funded. The only taxable portion of each $9,000 annuity payment Rob gets will be $3,000, because $6,000 of that came from the premium payments he made to fund the annuity. So, for a $60,000 investment, the final value of the annuity will be $90,000.

The return on this investment is low, so it appeals to people who do not feel comfortable with a high-risk investment strategy. A variable annuity is based on the same concept, but the funds are invested in the stock market, so the return depends on how the economy performs.

If you are self-employed, there is a retirement savings plan with a funky name for you. The Keogh plan — pronounced "key-oh" — is a qualified retirement plan for sole proprietors and partners, but it can also be used by your employees. The restrictions, distributions, and other details are similar to a defined-contribution plan or defined-benefit plan.

An individual retirement arrangement (IRA) is just what it sounds like: a retirement account you set up for yourself. There is a limit to the contributions you can make annually. There is a tax deduction for making these contributions every year, so technically they are tax-free contributions. The taxes come after you withdraw the money, at a time when you are in all probability earning less money, so the amount you pay will be lower — which is one of the main selling points for this kind of retirement investment. You can hold onto these funds until the age of 70 and a half, but after that, the payments will begin.

The next generation of the IRA is called the Roth IRA. Named after its primary legislative sponsor, Senator William Roth from Delaware, contributions to this IRA also are tax-deductible in the year they are made, and taxes are paid when the money is withdrawn. The difference is that the interest earned while the money is invested will be tax-free if you own the Roth IRA for at least five years. There are limitations on how you can invest the money in your Roth account and big penalties if you take the money out before five and a half years have elapsed, but you can begin distributions that early if you meet the conditions. The Roth IRA also has a distribution requirement that kicks in at age 70 and a half.

Like other tax laws, changes in regulations governing retirement-plan arrangements are enacted from time to time. Keep abreast of the status of your plans and any legal changes affecting them.

Your Government Nest Egg

Social security, Medicare, Medicaid: Most people have heard these terms and been told they compose a safety net for those who have absolutely no other resources on which to rely when they are no longer able to work or are legally entitled to receive government benefits. That regular Federal Insurance Contributions Act (FICA) deduction, painfully visible on every pay stub you have ever received, is what makes up these government benefits.

The Social Security Administration now sends out annual reports breaking down your contributions and an estimated payment that you are likely to receive, depending on the age you elect to begin receiving benefits. If you are not getting an annual report, you can go to **www.ssa.gov** and find your status. Even if you have not seen one of these statements, it is a safe assumption that the monthly payout will be insufficient to pay your bills after you retire. It is still important to have some understanding of how much of your money the government will give back to you and how it will affect your taxes, as well as the taxes your beneficiaries will pay (yes, social security benefits are taxable income).

Social security retirement benefits

The retirement income provided by social security, commonly referred to as an old-age benefit, depends on how many years you worked full time and paid into the system. If you meet the minimums — ten years of employment or 40 quarter-years — then you are considered fully insured. Those who have less than the minimum time in — younger people or those who have worked on and off over a long period — are called currently insured and only are entitled to disability benefits.

You can begin receiving old-age payments at a reduced benefit starting at age 62. If you wait to age 65 or later to sign up for benefits, you will receive more. If you decide to work while receiving benefits, the amount you receive can be reduced. There is an earnings limit for various age ranges. However, if you defer receiving your old-age benefit until later, starting at age 66, your payments will increase. These increments are stated in the report provided by the Social Security Administration.

Your social security payments do not have to be paid directly to you. You can designate a beneficiary for the full benefit or split it between you and another person. One-half of your payment can go to your current spouse, or you can designate an ex-spouse to whom you were married for at least ten years who has not remarried. Children also can receive half the payment while you are alive or 75 percent of the payment after you die; adopted children qualify, and under some circumstances a stepchild might qualify. Grandchildren and widows or widowers also can receive benefits as long as they meet specific criteria.

Part of this old-age benefit is a lump-sum payment to the surviving spouse or child of the deceased to help with funeral expenses.

Social security disability benefit

If you are unable to work and you qualify as disabled — there is a list of disabilities that, according to the government definition of the word, qualifies or disqualifies you — then you can receive social security disability payments until you reach 65. At that point, you begin to receive the social security retirement benefit at the same rate. The amount of money you receive depends on your work history, so there is no hard-and-fast number for this benefit. You can find more information at **www.ssa.gov/disability**.

Social security supplemental security income (SSI)

This benefit is for people who have very little (if any) property, or are blind or disabled in some other way. This is an absolute last-resort situation; it is good to know it is there if you need it, but doing everything possible to avoid that need is an excellent idea.

Medicare and Medicaid

These terms are not interchangeable, even though they both are a medical benefit. Medicare is a medical insurance program offered by the federal government to people who are 65 or older, certain disabled people under the age of 65, and anyone with permanent kidney failure. This last category was added in 1972 out of a concern that people needing life-sustaining dialysis might not be able to afford it. Part A of this coverage is hospital insurance, and Part B is medical insurance. Part B now comes with a monthly premium.

Medicaid is a state-run medical plan that is supported by federal funding and provides minimal medical benefits for the financially needy. To qualify for this plan, you only can possess a set dollar amount in property — $2,000 is a common limit, but different states set different caps for single and married people.

New Jersey's Medicaid program is available to persons age 65 or over, the blind, or persons adjudged disabled by the Social Security Administration or the Division of Medical Assistance and Health Services. The standard property-cap limit to be eligible is $2,000, but there are variables for different circumstances, such as whether a person is married, institutionalized or classified as "medically needy." Those in dire circumstances should check with New Jersey's Department of Human Services for qualification standards. Because medical bills can be extremely high, it is entirely possible that a serious illness could devastate your savings and make it necessary to take advantage of this program, so it is important to be aware of it.

Protecting Your Eggs

Estate planning is about protecting your property, and that includes the nest eggs and the baskets that hold them. In addition to estimating what money you will be spending from your retirement accounts, you need to consider what might be left in those accounts after you die. You need to do additional research to make sure what you expect to be there will be there.

Is your pension plan insured?

The Pension Benefit Guaranty Corporation (PBGC) is a federal agency that can insure and, therefore, protect some or all of your pension if your plan qualifies for the coverage and your company purchases the insurance. Not all pensions are insured and, if they are, they might only be insured for a percentage of each account. You should contact your employer's human resources office to find out whether your pension is insured.

Lump-sum payments

Be wary of any retirement investment that offers a lump-sum payment over annual distributions. This kind of plan assumes the company will be in business and have the necessary funds after you retire. However, given the way formerly "indestructible" investment institutions and financial companies have fallen falling, there is no guarantee.

Company stock contributions

If your company matches your retirement investments with its own stock, it is a good idea to diversify your holdings as much as possible. If selling your company stock is an option, most likely after you are fully vested, then consider doing that. Company loyalty is one thing; risking your financial security on any one company is a dangerous investment strategy — think WorldCom, Enron, and Bear Stearns. It is not about your commitment to your employer, but your responsibility for your own future.

Medicare supplemental insurance

Medicare is a wonderful benefit, but it is not perfect. There could be times when Medicare will not pay for treatments, medications, or doctors you need. If you have health issues, it might be a good idea to investigate and invest in Medigap insurance — an insurance plan specifically designed to pay for Medicare exclusions.

Beneficiaries and their taxes

Always name beneficiaries for any retirement resources you have. If you do not name a beneficiary and a substitute, then the money in those accounts will be added to your probate estate and be subject to the claims of creditors and taxation by state and federal governments. Also, make sure your beneficiaries know they have been named and what the tax implications might be if they receive those funds. You might decide to make sure your estate provides them with enough money to cover these taxes. *See Chapter 4 for information on taxes.*

Retirement/Estate-Planning Strategy

Now that you have an idea of the breadth and scope of retirement savings plans and the resources available to you through the U.S. government, you need to decide how to use or save your retirement money.

You can spend it all. You might want to completely exhaust all your retirement funds — after all, that might be why you saved all that money. That way, you do not have to worry about paying the bills when you want to stick your toes in the sand. Your remaining property is your back-up plan. Whatever is left when you die is what you leave to others.

Then there is the frugal approach — choosing to link your retirement needs and spending with your estate planning so that you estimate what you will need until you die, then adding a cushion to preserve the bulk of your estate for your spouse, children, grandchildren, and others.

By using this last approach, you take into account tax payments and future security for the people and organizations that mean the most to you. This is much more work and adds other considerations, such as inflation and keeping up with tax laws. However, it is your money, and if you want to have a say in what happens to it when you no longer have a voice, then this is the best way to do that.

CASE STUDY: RETIREMENT ACCOUNTS AND ESTATE PLANNING
Howard McEwen, CFA
Makris Financial Group, Inc.

How much of an impact does a retirement account make on an overall estate plan?

It is important to remember that a will does not dictate the beneficiary of retirement plans, such as 401(k)s and IRAs.

The owner of each of these types of plans is allowed to designate a beneficiary. How the beneficiaries are treated is laid down by the 401(k) or IRA's custodial agreement. This custodial agreement overrides anything a will has to say.

Owners should do and look for the following:

- Make sure they designate a primary beneficiary — who gets the money when you die.
- Make sure they designate a contingent beneficiary — who gets the money if you die and your primary beneficiary is also dead.
- Make sure that the custodial agreement allows a per stirpes designation. "Per stirpes" means that if one beneficiary dies, that beneficiary's heirs will be entitled to those assets.

- If needed, make sure beneficiary restrictions can be put in place. If someone is young or has special needs, getting a large chunk of money at your death might not be best for them.
- Regularly review beneficiaries and make sure you have records of who they are — and let your heirs know where those records can be found.

Any negative impact on estate planning is not tremendous if the retirement accounts are managed properly. The primary thing is to keep beneficiary designations up-to-date.

For example, take my client Johnny Jones, who came to my office several years ago. Johnny is a widower in his late 70s. He had a daughter and two sons. His daughter, Irene, was married with two children. His eldest son, Max, was married with three children. Bob, the baby of the family, never married and had no children. Bob also had some brushes with the law and is still wrestling with addiction problems.

Johnny retired from a large Fortune 500 company after 30-plus years of work. His main asset was his 401(k) plan that he rolled over into an IRA when he retired. Johnny did not give much consideration to designating a beneficiary. In fact, he did not remember discussing it with his advisor.

After growing dissatisfied with his old advisor, Johnny came to my firm. Unfortunately, his eldest son, Max, had died in an industrial accident three years previously. I noticed on his current statements that Max was still listed as a beneficiary.

"Yeah, I just hadn't gotten to that yet," Johnny said.

After looking over the custodial agreement, I explained what would happen to Johnny's money if he happened to die without updating it.

"The custodial agreement doesn't provide a per stirpes provision," I told him. "What this means is that if you die right now, only Irene and Bob will get any money. Max's children will be totally disinherited."

"You mean, even though he's still on there, his share won't pass on to his children?"

"Right," I said. "If Irene and Bob decided to disclaim a portion (basically say, 'I don't want Dad's IRA'), Max's children might inherit — if the courts decide that way. But there are no guarantees that Irene and Bob or the courts will carry out your wishes in this case."

"Also, how will inheriting a large sum of money affect Bob? He's already dealing with addiction issues. Could getting this inheritance actually kill him?"

These are blunt questions with a simple answer: Keep an updated beneficiary designation form, designate those beneficiaries per stirpes, and restrict what kind of money Bob would inherit.

Is there anything a person can do to maximize their retirement plans?

I consider two ways to maximize a client's retirement plan. First is pre-death, by properly allocating a client's account with regard to their risk-reward profile. The second is post-death.

Here is how: In the custodial agreement of an IRA or 401(k), a client should verify that his or her beneficiaries can perform a stretch IRA.

For the majority of Americans, an IRA or 401(k) is their largest asset. By stretching that IRA across multiple generations, an IRA owner can create tremendous wealth for future generations of his or her family.

How do you stretch an IRA? Simple: by withdrawing the absolute minimum necessary to meet IRS regulations. The funds that remain in the IRA are allowed to compound tax-deferred over a number of years.

Here is a simple example:

David Johansen is married to Patty. They have one son, Sami. Sami has a daughter — Chrissie, age 1, the apple of her grandparents' eyes.

Sami is financially self-sufficient, so David designates Chrissie as the sole primary beneficiary on one of his IRAs, an IRA that Patty will not need if he should die.

In the year David turned 70 and a half, the IRS mandates that he withdraw a percentage of his IRA. In that first year, the withdrawal is 3.65 percent.

David takes this withdrawal and then dies.

Chrissie becomes the owner of that IRA, now worth $100,000. Because it was her grandfather's IRA, she is still required to make withdrawals, but those withdrawals are based on her age — not her grandfather's.

Thus, that first year, 1-year-old Chrissie would have to withdraw $1,225. The IRS tables provide a life expectancy of 81.6 years for Chrissie, so $100,000 / 81.6 years = $1,225. If the IRA earns an average of 8 percent over Chrissie's life expectancy, her grandfather's IRA would have paid her $8,167,629.

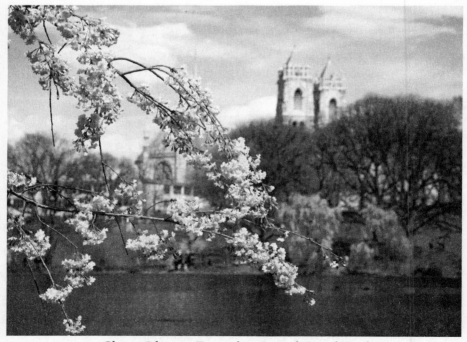

Cherry Blossom Festival in Branch Brook Park

CHAPTER 9

Setting Priorities

Estate planning is more than just deciding what to do with your stuff after your death. Some thought needs to go into what you want to do and how you want to try to prepare for the things you can and cannot predict. A crystal ball to look into the future is wishful thinking, but an even better resource is close at hand — the past. By making time to review the decisions and choices you have already made in your life, you can see what has been important to you.

When you had an opportunity to invest in your 401(k) at work, did you put in the maximum amount allowable or a modest percentage of your income — or did you defer investing until later? Are you glad you made the choice you did, or would you do things differently based on what you now know?

The answers you come up with are an example of how to begin making some decisions. By looking at what you used to think about financial matters, the change in the mix of people in your life, and the organizations you used to support, you can see patterns or inconsistencies that are important to the priorities you set for your estate.

This review also needs to include your current financial situation. The credit card debt you do or do not have is influenced by your view of the use of credit. If you do not have any credit cards, that says something about your views on the use of plastic for making purchases and whether paying interest on a purchase is acceptable. Maybe you have a small balance because in the same month you had replaced the tires on your car, the bottom of the water heater dropped out, and you simply did not have the cash to pay for a new one. Paying off that balance right away or letting it ride for a bit until you get back from your next business trip also says something.

It can be fun to reminisce about the unexpected adventure to South America with a college course you only took because of that cute guy or girl you thought you wanted to date. It also can be difficult, even painful, to remember a family beach vacation that ended up with Grandpa in the hospital and dying three months later. But if you make the effort, you might recall how much fun he had preparing for and involving you and the other grandchildren in the crab boil at sunset, and that will inspire a desire to share that experience with your grandchildren.

The essential part of this process is being attentive to the insignificant, the significant, and everything in between. All these details can serve as helpful pointers now and potential visions for the future.

Your Own Who's Who

Even though every person in your life might not end up in your will, considering the people who are important to you, and those who are not, is one way to identify what matters most to you. Because you are considering your priorities for yourself in addition to your family, friends, and maybe even professional associates, a review of people connected to those priorities makes sense.

The most obvious important people are your family and closest friends. Most people can rattle off the names of people they are related to by birth, marriage, or mutual agreement — friends frequently become "chosen family." A bit more thought might be needed when considering extended family or distant relatives.

It might be a given that family is so important to you that everyone living in your house will sit down to eat at least one meal together every day, often dinner; children home from college or the grandparents visiting from out of state for a week all know this is expected. It might also be known by your children that there are some family members they never see but for whom everyone signs the family holiday card each year; if those same people send a note with a small gift for a birthday or graduation, a thank-you note will be written because those distant relatives are equally important. These relatives are always invited to parties even though they never come.

Priorities revealed:

- Time with family is more than important; it is essential.

- Every celebration that calls for a party begins with a call to family members to find out what dates work for them.

- Even though some relatives live far away or might even be reclusive, you make sure your children keep in touch; you want them to have a strong sense of family regardless of proximity.

Implications for estate planning:

- Immediate family is so important that you want to make sure they have what they need.

- A desire to leave something to every family member, be it cash or a memento.

- Is everyone clear about how important your family is to you? Just because family time and ties are important to you does not mean your siblings, children, or anyone else will be aware of this. Clearly communicating this priority to your family is a good idea so that when the will is read and the distant relatives are included, your wishes are carried out, and the immediate family does not contest your bequests.

People come and go from our lives at various times for different reasons. The people with whom you surround yourself now are probably a quite different mix than the mix of people from your past. Even though life circumstances play a part in that coming and going of people, the effort you make to include, or exclude, people from your life places a value on those relationships. If you go out of your way to call someone or delete a message from the answering machine with no intention of calling a person back, it says something about how you feel about that individual.

Looking at the changes in your personal circle is one way to approach this review of people. For example: After being widowed, you might have lost touch with your in-laws; this does not bother you because they never liked you or the fact that you married their son or daughter. The children are old enough to visit their grandparents when they want.

You remarried and have become close to the extended family of your current spouse. This new, blended family includes an alcoholic uncle you simply cannot stand to be around, even though everyone thinks he is the life of every party. Similarly, when your children get married, they do not want to have to juggle multiple Thanksgiving dinners because they embrace the blended family as positive and open. So, they propose a huge family gathering of all sides that results in meeting new family members with whom you now enjoy weekend camping trips and a weekly bowling league.

Priorities revealed:

- You want to have people in your life with whom you can have friendly, healthy relationships.

- You are willing to meet familial obligations, such as making an effort with your in-laws when your wife was alive, but after an obligation is fulfilled, you are all right with letting it go.

- Distancing yourself from people who can be harmful to you or your family is also all right, but you try to do it in a manner that does not upset others.

- Family is important but not exclusive; "biological family-only" events rarely happen because they feel exclusionary.

Implications for estate planning:

- Including people who are not related by blood in your will must be handled legally and carefully to avoid any contest after you are gone. State laws governing family inheritance are clear; the same cannot be said for state laws regarding nonrelatives.

- Leaving money to a family member with an addiction or some other life problem — maybe an abusive spouse or unscrupulous children — might require the use of a trust and a trustee to avoid potential disasters.

- Give consideration when not including someone in your will. Giving a significant bequest to a specific person might not sit well with you, but a small gift could be considered to avoid a contest resulting from complete exclusion.

People you call friends can change over time. For example: The college roommate with whom you shared many late-night study sessions and much burnt microwave popcorn moved from experimenting with drugs to hardcore use. The last time he called you to bail him out of jail, you told him it was the last time, and you have not heard from him since.

Then there are the people we encounter just doing our everyday business. We can easily take them for granted, not realizing their importance until something happens. For example, there is Betty, the elderly woman who lives down the street and has no family. She ends up in a nursing home after breaking her hip, ending your Friday morning tea-and-cookies visits. There is the librarian who knows you by name and suggests books you might like. And there is the mechanic who normally changes the oil in your car, but one day is not there when you stop in. His son is at the register and explains that he was feeling tired and needed a few days off.

Priorities revealed:

- Your awareness of and concern for others extends beyond your immediate circle to acquaintances.

- Frequenting local shops and businesses is important to you; you go out of your way to avoid impersonal, big-box stores.

- You prefer to be a part of the community in which you live.

- Neighbors matter.

Implications for estate planning:

- Continuing to support the organizations and institutions you appreciate and that have been a source of friendships for you, such as your local library, might be added to your list of bequests so that when you are no longer around to cast your vote for a levy or make a donation you can still help.

- The support you give to a family-owned business might not be significant, but something in your estate might be helpful to them: Your mechanic might appreciate the tools you use for fixing your car.

- Donating your book collection to the local library would make your family happy; they are not big readers, and it would be one less thing to handle when it comes time to sell the house.

By taking time to consider people, you will naturally think of memories and specific milestones in life that are related. The things you experience directly or simply witness also provide an opportunity to review your priorities.

Memory Lane

Looking back to the mundane as well as the amazing through the filter of estate planning makes it possible to see how the past can inform and even direct the future. If you see accumulated knowledge and financial resources as the means to adding some adventure and comfort to the later years in your life, not just gifts for others, then you can live unfulfilled dreams or expand on some wonderful experiences.

Consider that trip to South America: Would you have begged, borrowed, or gone into debt to have the extra month in the rainforest, knowing you might never have the chance to go back? Look at this year's vacation plan. Are you going anywhere near a rainforest? Would you consider changing your plans to return to that place south of the border? Are you disappointed you cannot change your plans? Would you like to go again if you could come up with the money for the trip? Or has the idea of some tropical disease soured you on that kind of adventure? Does a cruise ship that anchors off the coast and includes a one-day trip to the very edges of the greenery sound more like your idea of fun?

Any number of events from the past can underscore the priorities you had at that time and how far you have drifted into another view of what is important. Here are a few memory joggers to get you thinking:

Family time:

- Vacations only with immediate family or large, extended gatherings.

- Annual visit from the cousins was fun/torture.

- Having a sleepover at a friend's house made you want to stay there/go home.

- Thanksgiving dinner did/did not include a "kids' table."

- How many parties were held at your house, and which ones did you enjoy or loathe?

School:

- Favorite subject or class.

- Memorable teacher — the one who got you excited about learning and how he or she did that.

- The class bully and how you handled him or her when it was your turn to be picked on.

- Public or private? Liked or disliked? Why?

- Science fairs — participation by choice or force, and the level of desire to hide under your display table during judging.

- Fraternity, sorority, or independent thinker?

- Class office positions held by election or appointment.

Extracurricular:

- Scouting, or made fun of Scouts?

- Reporter for the school paper.

- Band.

- Helped teachers clean after school.

- Clubs.

- Sports.

Do-overs:

- Your first/second/third marriage.

- Rehabbing the cute bungalow that ended up selling for less than you paid.

- Studying economics and only taking one art class in college.

- Giving up your film cameras for digital.

- Donating your turntable and all your jazz record albums.

- Not touring Europe before having children.

These life experiences are more than just a reflection of how you used to feel or what you were forced into doing by your parents. Your recollections and the way you respond to them now are a measure of what matters to you now.

Maybe that beach house you rented in 1998 is exactly the kind of home you wanted to have when you dreamed of living in a beach house. Perhaps that dream is never going to come true, given the circumstances of your life, but there is still time to make changes right now. You have eight more years until you are fully vested in your pension fund, so you have eight years to plan. Prepare to sell your existing home and help your children deal with the shock of your move to Nags Head, North Carolina, and get your finances in order. Your accountant and lawyer can get to work on the papers for the living trust you need to make sure your retirement years will be nonstop beach time.

If having fun in your life was something you passed up to fulfill obligations or deferred to achieve other goals, then you might decide recreation is so critical that you want to share that lesson with your grandchildren. One way to do this is to make sure they have the "mad money" necessary to fund the fun: Set up a "mad money" trust for each grandchild to do whatever they want in the summer between high school and college. After you make that a priority — because their parents have already funded their tuition and other fees — you can figure out how much you need to save or how much you need to not spend from your retirement account to fund those trusts.

Reminiscing often includes groups of people with like-minded views and dreams. Those groups also matter when it comes to estate planning.

Your "People"

Not everyone has an entourage of groupies, support staff, and employees to do their bidding. More often, you are the one doing the work, and frequently it is for a nonprofit organization. Your priorities about which causes or institutions to support have most likely changed over the years. The arts, once a luxury on a limited budget, are now at the top of your annual giving list, but the Peace Center that was struggling to survive in the basement of the dilapidated building next to your first apartment has moved to the storefront and still gets 20 hours of your time every month.

The institutions that rely on your time, money, or donations of office supplies have captured your imagination or hopes, or maybe just inspired you with their underdog determination. Whatever the reason, they are important to you. While they consider you among their supporters, one of their people, the fact is that your desire to see them succeed makes them your people.

Considering the nonprofits you have supported at different times in your life might spark an interest to get involved or lend support again. Life changes; a parent dying of cancer might inspire you to add the American Cancer Society or a hospice to the list of charities you wish to support.

Because estate planning is more than distributing belongings after you die, the importance you place on these groups needs to be factored into your priorities. Maybe the Peace Center is on the verge of needing to move because it is growing rapidly. Or perhaps that old bakery building you bought a few years ago has not turned out to be the successful investment property your real estate agent swore it would be; putting it into a charitable trust or making an outright donation of it to the Peace Center might be the best way to help it and reduce the amount of real property in your estate.

If you do move to that beach house in Nags Head, the time you spend at the cat rescue shelter is no longer going to be an option. You know it desperately needs volunteers, but even more desperate is a need for cat food. A donation of cash for the purchase of food is only going to be possible if you set up a way to make it happen.

After you fund the mad-money trusts, make sure you have enough to live on during retirement and cover the cost of your disability insurance as the safety net; it might be that you only have enough in your estate to support two charities. Which will they be — the arts organizations, the Peace Center, or the cat shelter? Do you want to set aside a little extra in case you find an institution in Nags Head you might want to support?

These are the difficult decisions that must be made if you prefer not to work extra hours or cut into your current spending to allow for future expenditures.

Must-Do List

The things you never thought you would do in this life or the envious moments spent listening to others describe what you have always dreamed about doing inspire some people to create a must-do list. Be it mountain climbing or scuba diving, going out to dinner at a five-star restaurant, or taking two weeks off work to just stay at home and relax, the things you feel are important enough to put on a list are important enough to make happen.

Setting priorities for your estate planning is a means to that "must-do" end. Identifying what matters most right now and what you thought was important but now realize is no big thing makes it possible to consider financial decisions that will have an impact now and later.

CASE STUDY: A FINANCE COACH FOR ESTATE PLANNING

Sue Holm, Founder
Make Peace with Money
sue@makepeacewithmoney.com
www.makepeacewithmoney.com

How should a person make decisions about their priorities?

All major decisions about financial priorities should be made with a trusted advisor or counselor. For some folks, that can be family or friends. For some, that is a financial planner or advisor. If someone has emotional issues about money, a financial counselor, coach, or therapist who is comfortable with money issues should be consulted.

There is an element of spirituality that also touches these decisions during life and when contemplating death. How much to give away? To whom? Why? When? Charitable giving, tithing (donating a fixed percentage of income to a religious institution), and giving back are all rich issues for discussion — among families, faith communities, and in our world. Does charity begin at home? What does that mean? What does that look like? Is money good, bad, or neutral? Are money and spirituality linked or not?

How do people apply these priorities to their decisions about disbursing their money and property after their death?

By not planning, people allow the state to dictate the disposition of their money and property. For those who have priorities, familial or spiritual, those priorities will drive the nature of the disbursal.

Why do people fight over things like a toaster or a chair after someone has died?

Because they have unresolved emotional issues, either about themselves and their self-worth, or their relationship with the deceased.

How can the person who owns the toaster or chair prepare his family for that situation?

If people are clear about their intentions in creating estate plans and have the occasion to discuss their intent with their family, it can defuse some of the tension. The person who owns things can create an atmosphere in which it is OK to ask for what you want while they are still alive. They can ask their loved ones what they need or want as a remembrance. They can create a system for disbursing things not otherwise specified in the will.

How often should those priorities be revisited?

Financial priorities should be revisited at all major life milestones — marriage, divorce, birth of children, children achieving their majority (turning 18), and the birth of grandchildren.

What are the benefits of working with a financial counselor or coach?

The benefits include financial clarity, mastery, and ultimately peace with money. This manifests in decreased debt, increased saving, and earning what you are worth.

Many people do not know that financial counseling or coaching is available. Many people with financial issues know they need help; they just do not know how to find it. A lot of people think that because they are smart and successful in most areas of their life, they should know what to do with money, or that they will be able to figure it out themselves. This can be increasingly frightening and frustrating as they try and fail on their own.

Among the most productive discussions between a financial counselor and client are those that involve the differentiation between needs and wants and how to prioritize them.

How should a financial professional collaborate with other people in an estate-planning team?

Ideally, during the financial counseling process, the counselor will refer the client to an estate-planning professional if the client does not yet have an estate plan.

Financial counselors can be an excellent resource for estate-planning professionals working with surviving spouses or partners who need or want some structure and support while they assume financial responsibility for themselves or for the estate.

Additionally, estate-planning professionals should consider referring clients who inherit sums of money or assets they are inexperienced in managing to a financial counselor.

How does a person go about choosing a financial professional? What characteristics or experiences should a client look for?

As this is not a licensed or regulated field, it is important that clients examine the credentials of anyone they are considering as a financial counselor or coach. Training agencies, such as the Financial Recovery Institute **(www.financialrecovery.com)**, frequently list those counselors or coaches who have been trained and certified.

Many clients seeking financial counseling have not talked about their money issues with anyone. They frequently have conscious and subconscious money secrets. It is imperative that clients trust their financial counselor, and that a financial counselor or coach be able to deal with a client's emotional issues that underlie the money issues.

CHAPTER 10

Choosing Who, What, How, When, and Why

Now that you know what you own or need to save, and have an idea of what you will need to keep for yourself as you go forward, as well as a sense of the people and organizations you would like to support with your hard-earned assets, it is time to put all that information together into a comprehensive estate plan. *The detailed overview of the choices you have for delivering assets provided in Chapters 5-8 is just that — an overview.* The legal restrictions and limitations of different kinds of trusts, annuities, insurance policies, and other financial vehicles will help you identify potential resources that will meet your goals. Only professionals in estate planning can make your estate plan meet your goals and be legally binding.

Beyond the difficult choices of who gets what, you also need to choose the CPAs, lawyers, financial advisors, insurance agents, and others who will be a part of your estate-planning and management team. Many of these people receive commissions for the "sale" of different kinds of products. The trust that might be best for you could have a smaller commission than the trust with plenty of extras — a planner who is doing his or her job will suggest what is best for your needs, not his or her checking account. Even though a less expensive firm might be attractive while you are still building up your estate, consider the longevity of the firm; there is the distinct possibility that later you will have a larger estate if you get proper guidance.

Something with such a long-term impact as your estate planning deserves a high level of care, thoughtfulness, and attention.

Who and When: The Matching Game

The solitaire game Concentration, referred to as "the matching game" by many preschoolers, involves placing all the cards in a deck upside down on a table in a grid pattern. Each player turns over two cards; if they do not match, then they are flipped back over, and the next player takes a turn. The goal is to keep flipping over cards and remembering where each one is so that you can make matches — two fours, two queens, two eights — until all matches are made; the person with the most sets of matches wins. It is a good way to teach children how to increase their concentration skills, but the premise of the game is also a good method for distributing your estate. The key difference is that you decide what makes a match.

If you are unsure of how to begin, consider the sticky-note method. Put the name of each person and institution you wish to support with your estate; include yourself in that list if you plan on creating a living trust or dedicating other resources to your retirement that will be a part of your estate plan. In the case of multiple beneficiaries — you benefit from a living trust during your life and have a beneficiary for that trust after your death — be sure to note both people.

Make a sticky note for each asset that you listed on the Your Estate in Black and White worksheet. *This worksheet is located in Appendix A.*

Then get the Prioritization worksheet, also located found in Appendix A. Now you can compare what you think you want against the practical structure of the estate you are crafting by matching your sticky notes with corresponding items on the Prioritization worksheet. See whether the matches are what you want them to be..

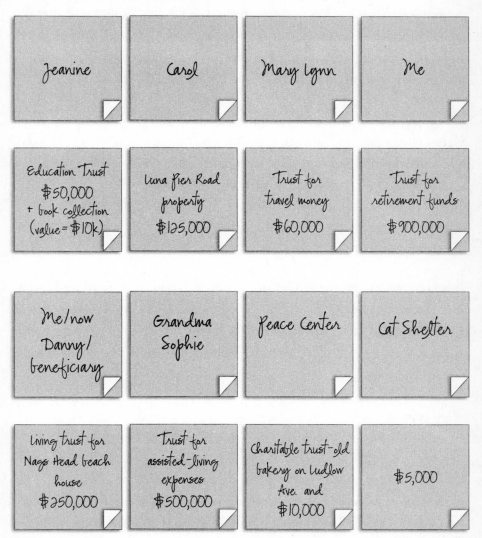

This method gives you a chance to see the differences in the amounts, property, and other bequests you make. This side-by-side comparison might also raise questions about the implications of the distribution.

Carol tends to be a black-and-white kind of person, so she might get upset when she learns the difference in the value of the property she gets and the Nags Head property going to Danny — the property she gets is worth 50 percent less. The fact that her profession is rehabbing houses and that she can invest a small amount to make the property equal in value — if not more — is something you might want to explain. Or you might decide to add some fixer-upper cash to her bequest to soften the blow.

You might not feel right about giving Jeanine a $50,000 bequest when Mary Lynn is getting $60,000, even though you know it is what they need. Add a little something to Jeanine's bequest if that makes you feel better.

But then, all these differences might not bother you in the least. You know what you are doing and why, and because it is your estate plan, the issue of fairness is a moot point.

This exercise also can provide an opportunity to consider bundling or separating items in your estate as part of a bequest. If you are looking only at the dollar value of a gift, packaging together the sentimental items with stocks, bonds, or cash will give you a chance to customize a bequest to the person who receives it.

Mary Lynn is not a reader, so the book collection would not mean as much to her as Jeanine, who is getting her degree in creative writing.

The charitable trust for the Peace Center that includes the old bakery is an incredibly generous gift — the largest it has ever received. That being said, the actual expense of the upgrades needed to meet building codes will take a big chunk out of the center's operating budget. The extra $10,000 can be invested until the Peace Center is ready to do the work, and it is also a way to motivate other donors to kick in some support.

It is not necessary to use sticky notes for this exercise, but it is important to note that a light breeze could blow away your efforts. Imagine how an overly enthusiastic pet can scatter pieces of paper that do not stick. A large dry-erase board or chalkboard serves the same purpose. Regardless of the method, the ultimate goal is simple: Match your priorities with the people and gifts you wish to give.

After you have settled on who is getting what, taking a digital photo of your makeshift plan could be helpful for later when you decide you want to make changes. *See Chapter 12 for more information on keeping your estate plan current.* You will have a record of your notes and can use that to reconstruct and revisit this process, or maybe you will want to show it to a financial advisor. Converting this information to an electronic document is a possibility by using a table in a word-processing document or using a spreadsheet program.

An estate plan is something you will need to regularly revisit and change, so consider keeping your notes and other planning documents for a while, at least until you are sure you have all the information saved in some other format.

When: Today, Tomorrow, or Later?

An important strategy for estate planning that goes unused by many is early gifting. The traditional or customary time for distributing an estate is after a person dies, but staying with the traditional can mean a larger estate and more taxes. A gift tax might still apply to the property you hand over early, but, given the rate of tax increase, it is entirely possible early gifting could mean a lower tax bill for the beneficiary.

Another thing to consider is when the beneficiary will get the most benefit from the gift you make. Your estate is yours to dispose of how and when you choose; if you want to take advantage of an opportunity to help a relative or charity in need, then you can factor that into your estate plan.

Jeanine graduated from high school with an International Baccalaureate (IB) degree — a special education program offered by her high school. She has changed her major in college from creative writing and is now majoring in political science. The whole family thinks she is making a bad decision and that she is too young to understand how she will be limiting her career choices to politics only. "Why be a politician? Everyone knows women can only go so far before they hit a glass ceiling," they think.

You see the potential Jeanine sees — and more. International corporations, government embassies, and a long list of opportunities await the person who has the background and understanding of multiple cultures and knows how to navigate the intricacies of governmental policy and social mores.

The cultural club she belongs to is planning a trip to Mongolia, and she desperately wants to go, but her education trust fund will not cover the expenses of the trip. She can legally go on the trip, but she does not have the cash. Because you want to encourage her passion and efforts to get a well-rounded education, not to mention some invaluable experience before graduation, you decide to create an education trust for Jeanine that specifically covers the cost of school-related travel.

Even though Jeanine will not receive any other money from your estate, you can remind yourself that she is getting an immediate benefit that will have long-term implications for her ability to build her own estate. It might be helpful to explain this to her, too.

Choosing to give some gifts early, putting conditions on other gifts, and explaining the logic behind why you are doing these things all need careful consideration. If your family is competitive or has some other characteristics that could inspire resentment or other negative reactions — before or after your death — you might want to consider sharing your reasoning. This can be done in the form of a letter to each family member that will be opened after your death, or at a one-on-one meeting in which you discuss the terms and conditions of your will and estate.

Regardless of how open or confidential you are about your financial matters, remember that after you are gone, your ability to explain yourself is limited. When deciding on the timing of your gifts, keep this in mind.

How: The Professionals

You can choose your estate-planning team from a host of people. Who does what and areas of specialty can get confusing. A CPA can address tax issues, but so can a lawyer who specializes in tax law. Who is better will depend on your needs. *See Chapter 2 for descriptions of important people who make up estate-planning teams.* Please refer to this chapter for a review of the parties.

The best way to determine who can help you with your estate planning is to look at your needs, preferences, and expectations. If this book is the extent of your estate-planning knowledge, then you have much to learn before you can check "estate-planning documents prepared" off your to-do list. A professional with access to multiple resources of current information that is written for the consumer and who has the patience to answer questions will be essential for you. Someone who does not knows what a QTIP is without looking in the glossary might prefer to seek a professional who can provide more detailed information without getting overly technical.

Beyond that, the circumstances of your life and interests will impact the time you have to spend, your level of commitment to achieving whatever timetable you set for completion, and the people with whom you work. Traveling across town for meetings might not be possible if you are caring for your 18-month-old twin nieces while your sister returns to school.

Some factors to consider before you begin putting together your estate-planning team are:

- **Interest level:** If a root canal without anesthesia sounds like more fun than estate planning, or you have a true desire to plan but lack the time to make it happen, then you have some sense of how much you do or do not want to engage in this process.

  Consider that 75 percent of Americans do not do comprehensive estate planning before they die, but the U.S. and state governments have enough laws on the books to take control of and benefit from your lifetime of work and savings. Focus on the benefits of this hard work, and consider the good things it can accomplish for you and those who matter most to you.

- **Deadlines:** Any significant milestones that are coming up sooner or later.

  If you have a three-month world tour planned for next year, it would be a good idea to get this process wrapped up before you leave the country. If you are not going anywhere for the next few years, you can take this process at a slower pace.

- **Health issues:** Even if you are healthy right now, your age and family medical history could impact your planning timetable.

  Grandma Nan lived to be 100, but all her sisters died of breast cancer in their 60s, and you are age 48. Your father-in-law died at the age of 40 of a massive heart attack, and your husband is 48 years old.

- **Family matters:** Collaborative relationships, disagreements, a marriage or birth, long-standing feuds, addiction struggles, helping with child care, and everything in between can impact your decision-making and the time you can commit to estate planning.

The bickering between two siblings might inspire a desire to cut them both out of your will, while a newly married couple means one more person to add — maybe two, if baby makes three.

- **Charities:** Like families, organizations go through considerable change. Insignificant change, such as a staffing change, or significant change, such as building a new facility, could influence your time commitment to estate planning, in addition to your giving.

The Friends Meeting House where you study received the permits and approvals necessary to go forward with the construction of its new building ahead of schedule; instead of breaking ground in five years, construction begins in eight months. You may need to revise when the Friends Meeting House will receive the money you intend to leave it.

After you have made up your mind to follow through with this estate planning you have been avoiding, and you know what your schedule looks like — as much as anyone can — you need to consider the components and status of your belongings. If you are just beginning to build your estate, creating a will requires fewer professionals than for someone who has 32 years in the workforce and multiple resources to consider. Special circumstances can complicate the process for any estate of any value.

The following offers an example of the many factors that may come into play when developing your estate family.

Family:

- Blended: His, his, hers, hers, and ours
- Unconventional: Same sex, interracial
- Adoption: Domestic or international
- Foreign-born spouse: Not a U.S. citizen

Personal:

- Career changes
- Multiple relocations: Domestic or overseas
- Frequent layoffs
- Mental health concerns
- Felony arrest(s)

Income:

- Structured settlements
- Rental property
- Inheritance
- Royalties
- Unemployment

Outgoing:

- Child support
- Alimony
- Elder care for parents
- Terminal illness

Whether these things affect you or your estate, they need to be taken into consideration. In addition to being information your estate planner will need to know — the firm you approach might not want to deal with estate issues related to people who are not U.S. citizens — they might have implications for your budget.

The adage "You get what you pay for" is a good rule of thumb for the level of risk you take with your estate-planning team members if you make decisions based exclusively on the fees they charge. It is entirely possible you will get lucky with phone-book roulette and stumble across a CPA who has your best interest at heart; and even though he has considerable experience, he is willing to charge next to nothing for his expertise because he wants you to keep your money. But the high-priced estate-planning firm, with more credentials than you have ever seen, is not necessarily going to give you the kind of service you need or collaborate with your other estate-planning partners.

The process of selecting the professionals with whom you will work requires some scrutiny of individual professional standards — credentials for a CPA, passing the bar exam (or not) — but some general expectations for this group of people can be defined. Consider the following when choosing a professional to assist you with your estate plan:

- Do you recognize the name of the school from which he or she graduated? What does this person do to stay current with changes in financial markets?

- How many years of experience does this person have?

- What is the focus or areas of expertise for that experience and the duration in each area?

- Does this person have a private practice, group practice, or corporate environment? Find out whether the expertise of others is readily available if a question or problem arises.

- Ask the Better Business Bureau and allied professional associations — such as the American Bar Association (ABA) for lawyers — for complaints, reprimands, or any other questionable business practices.

- Ask about the nature of relationships with the providers of the products the individual or firm offers; ask for a disclosure of commissions and other perks provided to the individual professional or firm.

- Review the website for current clients. Does the list include people with estates similar to yours, or are they high-worth individuals and business owners? A firm that specializes in businesses might do personal estate planning as an aside for those companies, but that is not its area of expertise.

- Talk to previous and current clients or friends and associates who recommend, or are wary of, the person and/or company.

After you have a short list of people to interview for your estate-planning team, prepare as much information as possible in advance of your first meeting. This step will help you and the professionals you interview to quickly determine how they might, or might not, be able to help you craft your plan.

CASE STUDY: ESTATE-PLANNING CHOICES

Scott J. Malof, CPA/PFS
SS&G Financial Services, Inc.
Certified Public Accountants
and Advisors * www.SSandG.com

What information should a person collect to prepare for this process?

When preparing for the estate-planning process, people should begin preparing a snapshot of where they are today. Create a family tree of personal details including ages and health status for immediate family members, as well as those whom you might have to care for, such as an aging parent. Also remember guardian nominations for your minor children, trustee nominations that are part of a will or other estate options, executor nominations to execute your will, separation/divorce agreements, and tax returns for the past couple of years.

This snapshot should include all relevant financial information, including listings of assets and liabilities, details of all insurance policies, and current and future income streams. Your financial situation would include a detailed personal balance sheet listing all assets and liabilities, life insurance policy details, other insurance coverage such as disability coverage, and income and expenses now and in the future.

The last piece, and often the most difficult, is your goals and expectations, including legacies.

What are the most overlooked loopholes or opportunities people miss when coordinating the financial aspect of their estate?

Here are a few:

- Not using up each spouse's applicable exclusion amount, both at the federal and state levels. For example, you could leave everything to your spouse.
- Assuming the children can divvy everything up fairly without fighting. This could be a mistake, not an opportunity.
- Not using a gifting plan.

How does the power of gifting affect an estate plan?

Currently, all individuals can give any other individual up to $12,000 annually without using up their lifetime applicable exclusion amount of $2 million. To the extent given away, this money is not included in the donor's estate at death.

Suppose a couple has two children, two surviving parents, and four grandchildren. This couple could give away $192,000 annually — eight people times $12,000 in gifts times two donors. If this were done for 20 years, the donors could remove $3.84 million from their estate, excluding the impact of earnings over those years. This couple could have a taxable federal estate at the highest rate, which is currently 45 percent. This process would result in a $1,728,000 savings.

The downside to gifting is relinquishing control over property. Also, giving large sums of money to minor children does not come without ramifications, both good and bad. This is why estate planning can be difficult for many people. The answers are not always about saving the most money or passing down the most wealth. It truly comes back to meeting a person's wishes.

How do state laws and federal laws affect estate-planning choices?
Federal and state laws have an enormous impact on estate planning. When people are determining where they would like their property ultimately to go, they need to be cognizant of the legal ramifications of their choices. For example, the rules for the transfer of property in a community-property state vary from those in a common-law state. Knowledge of these rules will help people plan accordingly.

Also, much of estate planning includes trying to minimize any transfer taxes that may come due. The amount of potential federal and/or state estate or gift tax has an enormous impact on the estate plan. For example, a couple with a $10 million estate could easily save more than $1 million with some simple estate-planning techniques. If this couple implements a gifting plan over a number of years, the savings possibility goes up substantially. Currently, the highest federal estate tax rate is 45 percent, leading to quite a savings when the estate is properly managed.

Confidentiality is important to many people — sometimes from the general public, but also from other family members. State laws in particular govern what information must be made public record through probate or disclosed on a limited basis, such as through trust reporting to beneficiaries. Clients need to determine how much they want the public or their heirs to know about what they have, how they are passing it on, and to whom.

CHAPTER 11

Planning Your Estate: Last Will and Testament in New Jersey

As mentioned in our general discussion in this book, specific requirements for drafting valid wills are directed and controlled by the laws of each state. While there are common principles, not all states are the same. It is always advisable to obtain legal counsel to assist you in drafting your last will and testament, especially if you have more than one residence in different states, or if you draw up your will in a different state than where you live. You should consult an attorney to ensure your will conforms to the proper controlling state law, as it will likely differ in various states. Additionally, state laws change from time to time.

Thus, it is important to understand New Jersey's statutory requirements for valid wills at the time you draft yours. Otherwise, your efforts to bequeath your property could fail; regardless of what you wrote down as your intent to distribute your property according to "your will," it will be the same as if you wrote nothing. You will have died intestate — without a will. In that event, your property will be distributed according to state law, possibly in ways you never imagined, and often at greater court costs.

According to current New Jersey law, any person age 18 or older and of sound mind is competent to make a will.

Sound mind means you know who and where you are, and your place in time, with an understanding of what you own. People are presumed to be mentally competent to make a will absent evidence to the contrary. A will might be challenged on the basis the testator lacked mental capacity. This requirement of mental capacity to make a will has made it standard legal practice to begin a will with the words whereby the testator states that he or she is of "sound mind" in "declaring my last will and testament," or words similar. These words of legal art make clear the intent of the document to be your will and further declare your recognition of the requirement to be of "sound mind and memory." Stating the exact words "sound mind," which quotes the New Jersey statute, is the best word choice.

Elements of a Valid New Jersey Will

In New Jersey, a will must be signed in writing by the testator and witnessed by two competent witnesses, unless the document qualifies as a holographic will. Unlike many other states, New Jersey allows a person who benefits from the will to act as a witness, as long as the person is generally competent otherwise to act as a witness.

Witnesses

Witnesses are a legal requirement for wills to be valid. Their necessity is highlighted especially in will contest actions. They could be called upon to testify to the circumstances of the signing of the will, the appearance of the testator as to soundness of mind, or that the testator signed the will him or herself in their presence or affirmed his or her signature in their presence.

One lawyer's anecdotal story illustrates the type of shenanigans that can take place with wills. The lawyer was called late at night by a client's son who asked him to come to the house because the client (the mother) was ill. The mother wanted the lawyer to witness her signing her new will and then take it into his custody. "Couldn't this wait until morning?" the lawyer asked. "She insists it has to be you," the son said, "and I'm not sure she will last the night." The lawyer, having served the client for many years, went to the house and was ushered into the woman's bedroom, where he found her propped on her pillows, a document before her on the bed, and a pen in her hand.

The son said to the lawyer, "Mother is having trouble speaking now, but I will help her sign the will, and we can both witness it." Whereupon, the son took the mother's hand and started to guide it upon the paper. "Wait a moment," said the lawyer, and he spoke to his client, who did not answer. He stepped closer and reached for her wrist. The son attempted to interfere, but the lawyer pushed him away and sought a pulse. As you may have now guessed, the mother had already passed away, and the son was attempting to get the new will signed posthumously, in hopes the lawyer would either be fooled or go along with it. Truth is stranger than fiction. Whatever the mother might have intended with the new will, she died before signing it.

Self-proving of a New Jersey will

New Jersey also provides form statements to be included with the will to make it "self-proving." The following form is prescribed by N.J. Stat. § 3B:3-4 to self-prove a will at the time it is made and executed:

"I, _____, the testator, sign my name to this instrument this _____ day of _____, 20____, and being duly sworn, do hereby declare to the undersigned authority that I sign and execute this instrument as my last will and that I sign it willingly (or willingly direct another to sign for me), that I execute it as my free and voluntary act for the purposes therein expressed, and that I am 18 years of age or older, of sound mind, and under no constraint or undue influence.

_____

Testator

We, _____, the witnesses, sign our names to this instrument, and, being duly sworn, do hereby declare to the undersigned authority that the testator signs and executes this instrument as the testator's last will and that the testator signs it willingly (or willingly directs another to sign for him), and that each of us, in the presence and hearing of the testator, hereby signs this will as witness to the testator's signing, and that to the best of our knowledge the testator is 18 years of age or older, of sound mind, and under no constraint or undue influence.

_____

Witness

_____

Witness

The State of _____

County of _____

Subscribed, sworn to and acknowledged before me by _____, the testator and subscribed and sworn to before me by _____ and _____, witnesses, this _____ day of _____

(Signed) _____

_____

(Official capacity of officer)"

New Jersey further prescribes the following form to be used to self-prove a will subsequent to the time it is made and first executed:

"The State of _____County of _____

We, _____, _____ and _____,
the testator and the witnesses, respectively, whose names are signed to the attached or foregoing instrument, being duly sworn, do hereby declare to the undersigned authority that the testator signed and executed the instrument as his last will and that the testator had signed willingly (or willingly directed another to sign for the testator), and that he executed it as the testator's free and voluntary act for the purposes therein expressed, and that each of the witnesses, in the presence and hearing of the testator, signed the will as witness and that to the best of his knowledge the testator was at that time 18 years of age or older, of sound mind and under no constraint or undue influence.

_____

Testator

_____   _____

Witness   Witness

Subscribed, sworn to and acknowledged before me by_____,
the testator, and subscribed and sworn to before me by_____ and _____, witnesses, this_____
day of _____.

_____

(Signed)

(Official capacity of officer)"

Changing Your Will – Codicils

You have made your will, and it is done. But along comes something new: Another child is born; new property is acquired or property is sold; a divorce occurs; a marriage happens; a death happens; or a loss occurs. Life changes. Whatever the reason, you decide you want to change something in your will, just one provision or part of it, or you just want to add something to it without changing the whole thing. A codicil is an addition you can write and attach to or put with your existing will. You may do this in New Jersey by following the same procedures required to make a formal will, with two witnesses, and designating it as a codicil to your will. If multiple codicils contradict each other, the most recently signed and dated codicil will be the provision that is considered valid. You also may make a fully handwritten codicil, as New Jersey recognizes holographic wills.

Holographic will

New Jersey is one of the few states that recognize a holographic will. This is a will written out in the testator's own handwriting and signed. Witnesses are not required.

Holographic wills also have been ruled to be legal when written on various types of substances. Ideally the testator would choose a high rag-content quality paper and an ink that can reasonably withstand the rigor of time, and then store the will in a safe place. Other quixotic things at hand have been used, such as shirts, wood planks, napkins, cardboard, paper scraps, and melon rinds. These will work if the controlling rules of testator's own handwriting, legibility, date, signature, soundness of mind, and intent to be a will are satisfied. It is said that Leo Tolstoy, the famous Russian writer, wrote out his last will and testament on a tree stump.

Nevertheless, unless decent pen and paper are unavailable in exigent circumstances, your last will and testament is not the place to express humor and eccentricity, not if you intend to make a valid and lasting will and not if you wish your mental capacity in writing it to be questioned out of context. If a shirt, a plank, a napkin, etc., is all that is available, and time is of the essence, of course that is a different situation — and you might say in the will, "This is all I have to write on."

Such exigent circumstances can be dramatically proved and are self-explanatory in some circumstances, where holographic wills are honored. Many such examples have occurred in heartrending situations on battlefields where the documents amazingly survived the chaos and destruction, often on bits of paper and even on helmets. One famous holographic will was written in Saskatchewan, Canada, in 1948. In a freak farming accident, a farmer named Cecil George Harris was trapped under his tractor wheel for ten hours; with amazing fortitude, he carved his will into the tractor's fender with his pocket knife. It read: "In case I die in this mess I leave all to the wife. Cecil Geo. Harris." Though alive when rescued by neighbors, Mr. Harris died two days later. The fender was removed from the tractor and filed with the court for probate. The court accepted it as his valid will. The fender and Mr. Harris' knife with which he carved it are now on display in the law library at the University of Saskatchewan College of Law, after having resided for many years in the courthouse.

Not only were Mr. Harris' exigent circumstances self-explanatory, but he had the incredible presence of mind to make it clear by referring to "this mess" in transcribing his simple will. Furthermore, there were witnesses, not serving as signatories to the will itself, but to its circumstances.

Oral will

Some states recognize oral, or nuncupative, wills declared by the testator in belief of imminent death. These wills are usually subject to specific limitations. New Jersey does not recognize them.

Where to keep your will

Keep your will in a safe place, but one where it can be found when you are no longer here. Many people deposit their will with the attorney who assisted in drafting it. This is not a bad practice, especially if the attorney or his or her firm is the legal fiduciary whom you wish to assist with the probate of your will. You could also keep the will in a home safe that is fireproof or with the person whom you have named as your executor or executrix of the will. What is not a good idea in New Jersey is to keep your will in a bank safety deposit box if you are the only person who has access to the box. The reason is that upon your death, access to this box will be restricted until estate papers are filed with the probate court and a fiduciary is appointed — a difficult process when your will is sequestered and unavailable in that very box. If you wish to use a safety deposit box for your New Jersey will and other property that you do not wish to be tied up at your death, be sure to have a co-renter on the box. Even then, it is possible the bank might restrict access upon notice of your death until the court authorizes access. For this reason, a safety deposit box is not the most efficient place to keep your original will.

One helpful procedure in New Jersey is the option of registering your will with the New Jersey Secretary of State's will registry. The will itself is not deposited, but its existence, date, and location are put on record for a $10 fee. You may file this yourself or through your attorney.

Will Revocation

A testator can revoke a will by writing a new one that is properly attested by witnesses. Also, a testator can destroy, tear, burn, or mutilate a will or direct another person to do it in his presence. Revocation by destruction would have to prove that the testator intended to revoke the will. If a prior will is not clearly revoked in all respects, New Jersey will read the new will and prior one together and will recognize any statements in the prior will that are not inconsistent with the provisions of the new will.

Beneficiaries, Debts, and Entitlements

Subject to certain limitations, you can leave your property and possessions to anyone you wish. If you disinherit your spouse or domestic partner, they have the right under New Jersey statute 3B:8-1 to take an "elective share" of one-third the net estate. If there are no children or only one surviving child, a surviving spouse is entitled to 50 percent of the estate. If you have more than one surviving child, your spouse is entitled to one-third of the estate. Your bequests can be proportionately distributed only after the spousal legal entitlement is first satisfied.

If you wish to disinherit one or more of your children, it is best to expressly say so in the will, even though the words might sound harsh in black and white. Omission by silence might raise a question of mistake and open your intent to dispute. Wills have been challenged successfully by children appearing who were presumed dead, who were not known to exist, or who were disinherited by simply not being named in the will. What the testator intended about these children was not clear; therefore, it was presumed the testator intended to include the child in the estate. New Jersey does recognize the possibility of an after-born child. This means that when making a will, you should anticipate there could be a child born to you or adopted after the will is made. If your will is silent about such a child that exists at the time of your death, the child will likely be entitled to a portion of the estate even though you have not said so in your will.

As a result, you are well advised to foresee these circumstances and either expressly state that Johnny is not receiving anything under the will, stating a reason, or give a token bequest to Johnny, such as $1. In some cases, a child is not included in an inheritance because he or she has already received their share during the testator's lifetime. In other situations, there are simply bad feelings. Your attorney will advise you on the best way to handle such situations if you wish. The important point is to understand that your intent must be clear and rational, to avoid ambiguity in both the will's provisions and your mental state.

You can name entities and charities in your will, of course. When it comes to pets, be careful how you handle this in New Jersey. If you make Fluffy a direct beneficiary, Fluffy is not a "person." One way is to name a person in your will as a beneficiary who gets ownership and possession of Fluffy, along with a sum of money for Fluffy's care. For obvious reasons, this needs to be someone you trust to care for Fluffy — someone with whom you have discussed this plan when you made your will. Also, you should have a contingency in the will for if you outlive Fluffy.

Bequests to Minors

Money and property of any significant value left to children under age 18 will be controlled by New Jersey's statute controlling gifts to minors, which adopts the Uniform Transfers to Minors Act/Uniform Gifts to Minors Act. Under this provision, property given or bequeathed to a minor — under age 21 — must be held in trust for the minor under the control of a custodian of the property. If you do not name a specific person to be the custodian of the property for the child until the child reaches age 21, the child's parent or guardian likely will be the custodian of your bequest unless you or the court names a different person.

For this type of arrangement, you should not leave the details to chance. Use the services of a New Jersey probate attorney to assist you in drafting these provisions to ensure your wishes are carried out in the way you intend. You may be better advised to create a trust for a minor during your lifetime, or a pour-over testamentary trust, depending on your circumstances, timing, and the type of property or extent of wealth involved. By setting up the trust yourself in advance, you exercise better control over the administration of the bequest.

Spousal and Family Allowance

New Jersey statute provides for a spousal and child allowance. Recognizing that most states provide for an allowance and/or other support mechanisms for surviving families that are charged against the estate's assets, you should prepare your will to account for this reduction of the estate. Legal advice is important in making this adjustment.

Intestate in New Jersey

Probate law does not permit a vacuum. Property must have an owner. If a person dies without a valid will, New Jersey law provides how the person's possessions — his estate — will be divided. The intestate succession statute in New Jersey lists a potentially complex scheme of who will inherit, depending on the survivors and their relationship to the decedent. A surviving spouse or domestic partner will take all if there are no surviving children of the decedent. How the property is divided if there are children will depend on whether any of the children also are a child of the surviving spouse or domestic partner. If there is no surviving spouse, domestic partner, or civil union partner, then the statute looks to children. If there are no children, the standing of certain other specified relatives — parents, grandparents, and step-children — might come into play. The value of the estate also will have a bearing on the division of the property. New Jersey's intestate succession laws will control the dispersal of your probate assets if your will fails in whole or in part for any reason.

Death Taxes

When making your will and planning your estate, be sure to consult with your attorney and tax planner about the tax impact on your estate. This also will vary from state to state. New Jersey revised its death tax laws in 2002, in response to a struggling economy, to provide for death and inheritance taxes. Wills and estate plans prepared previously to this revision should be reviewed with legal counsel to assess the impact of this legislation. One of the implications of the law is a lien on the estate assets for death and inheritance taxes, preventing transfer of property without the signed release of the state's Division of Taxation. Similar circumstances exist in other states.

How Your Will Might be Challenged

By now, you have an idea of the ways someone may challenge your will if you have not closed the loopholes when you prepared it. The ways such challenges most often arise are:

1. The document filed with the court is not a valid will because one or more of the following is missing: proper date, signature, or words indicating it is meant to be your last will and testament; it is not properly witnessed by at least two competent witnesses who are not beneficiaries under the will; or it does not meet the requirements of a holographic will.

2. You were not of sound mind when you wrote it.

3. Some part or all of the will does not comply with New Jersey law.

4. Someone appears who claims to be your biological offspring but who is not mentioned in the will.

5. Someone appears who claims to be your lawful spouse but who is not mentioned in the will.

6. Someone comes forward with a new will or codicil of a newer date.

7. The will is claimed to be a forgery or fraud.

If the will first presented to the probate court meets all the basic legal requirements — original document, dated, intent or agreement to be a will demonstrated, disposal of property contained within, signature, and proper witnesses to the signature — the court will presume the will to be valid until proved otherwise. The challenger can file another will or codicil for the court to consider and evaluate, or can challenge the will itself, but the challenger must present evidence.

Perhaps the easiest challenge to a will is producing a more recent one that exhibits all the legal requirements, but where two wills are brought into question, it will often rest on the testimony of witnesses, and sometimes a handwriting expert, to determine which is the true will. The one of most recent date will be the controlling will. When you make a new will, you automatically revoke all prior wills. When you make a codicil to an existing will, you only revoke a provision of the will that you are changing, not the entire will, because you are not making an entire new will when you prepare a codicil.

You can look ahead to potential challenges and prepare your will to prevent those challenges from having any effect on your wishes by preparing your will with the assistance of counsel to ensure it expresses your intent and meets the statutory requirements of a will.

A Different Type of Will – Your Living Will in New Jersey

A "living will" is not about dispersing your property and stating your final wishes at the time of your death. It is about having your own control over your body if an accident or illness puts you in a medical situation in which it is difficult or impossible for you to speak for yourself in the moment. With a living will, a person can put in writing that he or she does not wish to be placed on life support systems if terminally ill or permanently unconscious (coma). The living will concept does not have the teeth of enforcement in all states.

New Jersey recognizes the living will concept as an advance directive. It has two types of advance directives: (1) a proxy directive and (2) an instruction directive. You can have either or both types in place.

- **Proxy directive:** This is a durable power of attorney for health care, which is a document utilized to appoint someone to make health care decisions for you if you are unable to make them for yourself due to either a temporary or permanent condition. The person appointed is known as your health care representative. This person, also known as your proxy, is responsible to base his or her decision on what he or she believes you would want if you were able to decide or speak for yourself or in your best interest

- **Instruction directive:** This is the living will or advance directive. In this document, you provide direction to your physicians, health care providers, and family about the types of situations in which you will or will not want life-sustaining treatment given if you are unable to express your own decision at the time. You also can use this document to explain your beliefs, values, and general care and treatment preferences. The instruction directive guides your health care providers and family as to what measures to take or to refrain from taking on your behalf. It relieves them of making the decision and allows you to speak for yourself for those situations covered in the directive.

Appendix C has Proxy Directive and Instruction Directive forms provided by the state of New Jersey.

CHAPTER 12
Keeping it Current

Y ou have a will. All your trust documents are properly executed. Your brother has agreed to be your trustee, and your sister is his backup. Your cousin is your executor, with your aunt as backup. All guardians are on board. All your beneficiaries are alive and accounted for. Insurance policies are up-to-date. You have a living will and organ donation form in the hands of your doctor. All powers-of-attorney are ready, and your retirement is fully funded. But, unfortunately, putting together a comprehensive estate plan is just the first step. The good news is that the final step is less time-consuming.

The final step is to review your plan once a year or whenever there is a significant change that will affect your plan or beneficiaries. If you schedule a review when you change the batteries in your smoke detectors on the first day of spring or at the end of summer, you will have time to implement any updates that will take advantage of any changes in tax laws before the end of the fiscal year. The regular discipline means you can take care of little changes quickly instead of having to go through the arduous process of making many changes all at one time.

After the volume of work that went into this plan, it might seem that a once-a-year review is quick and easy, but for those who wish to wash their hands of the whole business, that might seem too frequent. Your perspective is relative, so following the advice of those who know is a good idea. Most estate-planning professionals will tell you it is not a good idea to make many small changes throughout the year; it could get seriously expensive and complicated. A decision made in the midst of a difficult experience — such as eliminating a beneficiary from your estate — could result in a domino effect, with additional changes necessary, which will cost more time and stamina than you might have available. Change your mind again later, and the process starts all over.

The annual review sets a specific time for addressing issues that come up throughout the year. It also keeps your estate plan in the back of your mind. Just as you need to remember to change the oil in your car or the engine will blow up, you need to make changes to your estate plan, or it will not work the way you want it to. Once your estate plan is in place, maintenance can be simple.

What Changes?

It is not difficult to imagine the implication of some common life changes. Marriage, divorce, death of a beneficiary, the birth of a child, or losing your job will mean obvious changes to an estate plan: changing beneficiaries, including or removing a spouse on ownership documents, and updating your name if you legally change it. Other changes will require thought and planning in order to make the necessary adjustments to your original plan.

Property:

- You give away or sell property specified in a will or trust.
- A natural disaster destroys or causes serious damage to a piece of real estate.
- You acquire a substantial amount of new property.
- Your home is robbed and property in your will is stolen.

Health:

- You or someone in your family is diagnosed with a life-threatening illness.
- You are hurt on the job.
- A parent becomes seriously ill and cannot afford medical care.
- The doctor gives you a clean bill of health, and you can go back to work.

Good news (with strings attached):

- Your daughter is accepted to Harvard but does not qualify for student loans.
- The adoption agency in Europe approved your five-year-old application, and you need to go pick up your son next week.
- Your trustee was transferred to Nepal with no set return date.
- Your wife received a promotion and you are moving to the West Coast, which is closer to her family.

Some of these situations could mean you need to take out a loan against your retirement savings, but others will involve the thoughtful work of choosing a new personal representative and getting the related documents updated. Immediate needs should be addressed as they arise, such as naming a new trustee before heading to Europe to adopt your son, but some things can wait. Figuring out how to pay for a Harvard education and the implications it will have for your estate will take time.

Check with the members of your estate-planning team to find out what types of changes they recommend be done as quickly as possible and those that can wait. Establish how you will communicate these things, such as e-mail notes to an assistant or a signed, original letter. Few finance-related companies will accept or execute directions transmitted in a voice-mail message, but a message that an e-mail is coming and asking for a call when it arrives might suffice. Also, most transactions are now legally authorized by fax.

After you are clear about the information you need to collect, make sure you are keeping track of those pieces of information throughout the year. Consolidate and organize the information that will make it easy for you and your estate-planning team to have what you need. Create a file folder, make a running list, or designate a desk in your drawer for estate-planning essentials.

Make a copy of the acceptance letter from Harvard, staple to the back a print-out of the tuition and fee schedule you pulled from the website, and scribble notes to yourself for reference later: "Transfer stock from living trust? Sell time share?" If you will hand over documents to your lawyer or CPA, be sure to keep a copy for your files; if his or her copies get lost or you need to discuss something over the phone, having a backup copy will make things simpler.

What Does "Maintenance" Look Like?

Your estate-planning team might be a group of two or 16 individuals in one or eight different companies. Regardless of their number, they are all likely to have an idea about how to coordinate your annual review, make changes, and handle documents. With that many people involved, the potential for disaster is only slightly limited by the fact that they all have a stake in making sure your plan remains intact and up to date. As the person with the estate, you need to decide what is most comfortable and reasonable for you.

A simple approach makes the most sense for something new — it will get complicated all by itself, so there is no need to help that along.

Make a list of each person in your estate-planning team along with their contact information, including company name and secondary contact. Then add the elements of your estate plan for which they are responsible.

The following is an example of how this contact sheet may look.

Pat Johnson, attorney at law
(Primary contact)
Dewey, Cheatum, and Howe
1234 Jokester Lane, Suite 6789
Trenton, New Jersey 55555
513-555-1234 – Office
513-558-1098 – Direct line
513-555-2345 – Fax
513-555-3456 – Mobile
513-555-4567 – Home/emergency

Gail Silver, attorney at law
(Secondary contact)
Dewey, Cheatum, and Howe
1234 Jokester Lane, Suite 6789
Trenton, New Jersey 55555
513-555-1234 – Office
513-555-9876 – Direct line
513-555-2345 – Fax
513-555-8765 – Mobile
513-555-7654 – Home/emergency

*** If neither contact is available, call the main number and explain the situation. The receptionist will find an alternate contact for immediate assistance. ***

Hours: M – F 8 a.m. – 6 p.m., Sat. — by appointment, Sun. — closed
Documents: Will, living will, and organ donation documents
Stored: Dewey's document vault

After your list is compiled, look over all the contacts and decide who would make the best point person or coordinator among the group. This person will serve as the top of the phone tree; in the case of a need or emergency, you only have one person to call who will inform the rest, so you only have to say things once. It is similar to a snow day: One parent has a short list of people to call to say that school is closed, and each of those people has a short list. This way, everyone finds out rather quickly that it is a day for sledding. In the case of your estate plan, if one meeting is preferred, then your point person will collect and prepare all the documents needed from each person on the team so that you do not have to run all over town. The person who takes on this responsibility might charge a fee, but when you are short on time, the convenience is well worth the investment.

Next, you need to choose a date for that annual review. If you only have two people to meet, you could schedule back-to-back appointments on the same day and take care of your work for the year. The timing of this review will depend as much on your goals for your estate plan as it will on the space in your calendar. If taxes are a primary concern, then schedule your review at a point in the year that will allow you to have enough time to review the changes and implement decisions to maximize your savings or minimize your payments. If trusts are a big part of your estate, then the same kind of review will be needed to address any changes in trust regulations.

The likelihood of having time to do a review at the end of the year might be unrealistic — trying to squeeze in the appointments necessary between holiday parties, shopping, visits by out-of-town family, and inclement weather in some parts of the country can be a challenge. But then spring is a busy time, too, with breaks in school schedules and getting ready for graduations and summer vacations. There are more uses of your time than you thought imaginable when it comes to setting up a review of your estate plan. Ask your advisors what they think.

Periodic updates each quarter might help define when the annual review should happen. If a new tax law is passed in February, then an update from your CPA in March will give you plenty of time to consider the implications before the annual review you schedule for early September — the children are back in school, and the holiday rush has not yet begun. This kind of attention to your plan throughout the year will make the annual sit-down less involved.

If you have your planners get in touch with you a month or two in advance of your meeting, in addition to reminding you that it is coming, this will allow you to give them some directions about documents that need to be prepared. Following are a few examples of what could be happening that would be important to pass along:

- Your daughter Elizabeth just had a baby — Jeremy Jason Wolf — so you want to create a trust just like the one you have for all the other grandchildren. He also needs to be added to your will.

- Grandma Sophie passed away unexpectedly the week after Jeremy arrived; something needs to be done about her trust for assisted-living expenses, and you need to consider suggestions about what to do with it. She also needs to be taken out of your will, with Grandpa George as the new beneficiary for her bequests.

- Kelley dropped out of business school to pursue an arts training program — will her education trust be able to cover her expenses, even though the apprenticeship-like institution is not accredited?

You could sit down and sign the necessary documents at your review. Some of your team members might regard the review as the time to go over all that information and later follow up with the document signing. Keeping your team in the loop about what is happening in your life is important so that they can manage your estate plan, but you need to make sure that communication, again, supports your estate-plan goals. An e-mail or phone call when something significant occurs might be essential. Then again, waiting might not make much difference to your plan; it could save you considerable hassle given the number of times you would have to make those contacts.

What to Go Over

You need to go over all elements of your estate plan until the documents and routine become familiar. *The worksheets in Appendix A are useful to help establish the components of your estate plan.* These might include:

- Will

- Living will

- Organ donor form/card

- Durable power of attorney

- Medical power of attorney

- Guardians for children

- Guardians for others

- Life insurance policies

- Disability insurance policies

- Other insurance policies

- Trust: For children

- Trust: For retirement

- Trust: For charity _____

- Trust: Living _____

- Retirement: 401(k)/pension

You also will want to consider your executor and trustees, their backups, and anything else people-related. The goal is to ensure that your documents reflect your wishes so that after you are gone your estate is disposed of as you want. It also helps the people you leave behind, so you need to address with your estate-planning team how to make sure these things happen.

Your Desk

Federal law requires individuals and businesses to retain documentation that supports tax returns for a specific number of years. Anyone who has had to go through an audit learns the hard way that this is not merely a guideline. Estate-planning documents could be considered more important than your tax records because they are the legal record dictating the disposal of your property, and what happens to that directly affects the taxes paid by your estate and every one of your beneficiaries. Stuffing these things into a cubby of an over-stuffed roll-top desk and forgetting about them is not wise. Imagine your family trying to find the name of your lawyer in such a mess.

How to organize your documents and information is a personal matter. One file folder of everything might suffice, whereas a separate folder for each estate-planning team member might work best. Or you might assign one folder per document so that the history of all changes is readily accessible. Whatever method you choose, be sure to include any information your family might need to access after your death. You should include the following information:

- **Contact information:** Company name, phone number, fax, e-mail address, and any other information that you use to manage these accounts

- **Payment information:** Account numbers, usual due dates, and method of payment for any bills — automatic deductions from your checking or savings; online bill payment via your bank, coupon book, and checks mailed

- **Debts/accounts:**

  o **Real estate:** Home mortgage, second mortgage, timeshare, vacation property, and investment property

  o **Loans:** Line of credit, signature loans, and credit cards

- o **Utilities:** Gas, electric, water, sewer, heating oil, telephone, cell phone, Internet service provider, and cable/satellite

- o **Regular payments:** Car payment, insurance, automatic deposits into savings or other accounts, magazine subscriptions, and newspaper delivery

- **Resources:**

  - o **Income:** Payroll checks, rental income, structured settlement, royalties, annuity payments, and retirement distributions

  - o **Bank accounts:** Checking, savings, and certificates of deposit (CDs)

  - o **Investments:** Money market accounts

The Essential Documents and Accounts Inventory worksheet in Appendix A will help you begin assembling this information. If you already keep individual file folders for these documents so that you have a place to put the stubs from the electric company or receipts from the company that delivers your heating oil, then indicate the name and location of the folder. Also note if there is a monthly payment book or the electronic delivery of notices instead of traditional mail delivery.

For the truly meticulous, it would be a good idea to have a centralized place for the original paperwork created when an account was set up, correspondences, and any other historical documents. When an executor of an estate is contacted about an outstanding debt, having access to this kind of information could make his or her job much easier.

Unfortunately, this kind of consolidation also makes it easier for a thief or unscrupulous family member to gain access to your assets. For this reason, it is important to keep these documents in a secure location. A fire-resistant home safe or locking file cabinet will make the materials readily available to you, but a greater challenge for someone else.

• *Did You Know?* •

If you want to be buried instead of cremated after you are gone, you need to let your wishes be known. A former queen of England prepared every detail of her funeral, including the conveyance of her coffin to the church and who would be invited to have a seat in a pew.

Another royal, not held in high esteem at the palace, died unexpectedly, so a funeral had to be prepared quickly. The good news is that just such a funeral plan was ready; the bad news was mostly for the former queen who planned it — all her work was going to be used by someone else.

Most people will not need a protocol book for their final arrangements, but having things done your way will require you to make your wishes known. Planning your own funeral could seem a bit morbid, but look at it this way: You plan your birthday party, so why not plan your last party, too?

One Last Motivator: Probate and You

One big reason to make sure your estate plan is up-to-date is for avoiding probate court, even though it is no longer the nightmare it used to be. The probate process is designed to settle your debts and distribute your assets when the proper legal documents are not provided.

After your death, your executor is required to file your will with the probate court in the appropriate jurisdictions. If you have homes in two states, this means filing the will with the probate court in each state. The laws in each state might be slightly different, but the process is fairly standard. The following are general laws relating to probate:

- If a person dies without a will, an administrator — or executor — is appointed by the judge. If the person dies with a will but does not use will alternatives, such as trusts, to distribute assets to beneficiaries, then the named executor guides the will through the court process.

213

- The court posts a notice of your death, most often in local and regional papers, to notify creditors of your death and allows for a period of four or five months for any claim to be made against the estate. Once the defined window of time is closed, no more requests for payment will be considered.

- The executor/administrator notifies all beneficiaries and creditors of the estate that the administration of the will is going forward.

- The executor/administrator collects all the assets and prepares a list or inventory. Court approval must be sought to sell any assets in order to pay debts or make bequests.

- The executor/administrator reviews and pays all outstanding debts.

- The executor/administrator pays all taxes.

- The executor/administrator distributes the remaining assets according to the order of the court.

If the individual dies intestate, the court will designate heirs. If there is a will and the probate process is used to settle the estate, then the court can also make orders about which of the beneficiaries receives what. If a particular asset that was identified as a bequest has to be sold to pay taxes, then the court might order that the beneficiary of that asset be given something else, or that the person gets nothing.

Circumstances that influence the probate process do arise, and how each court in various states handles these circumstances might differ. In the case of murder, most states, including New Jersey, will not permit someone who intentionally kills a person to inherit any portion of the deceased person's estate; this includes receiving the proceeds from a life insurance policy, trust, or other arrangement. These are called slayer statutes.

In the case of adultery or abandonment, some intestate laws will not allow the spouse who cheated or deserted to inherit anything from the estate. The evidence needed to make the case for either situation varies. One distinction is clear in most states: A missing spouse is different from abandonment. A spouse who has not voluntarily moved out but is gone without any explanation can be declared missing. Usually a period of years must pass before any legal action can be taken. The common law rule was seven years if there was evidence the missing person was exposed to some sort of peril.

State laws might vary on this time and basis for assumption of death. New Jersey law states that a person who is missing from his or her last known residence continuously for five years, without any contact or satisfactory explanation after diligent search or inquiry, is presumed to be dead at the end of that five years — unless there is proof of an earlier death. The family can then request that the person be declared legally dead, making it possible to probate a will, receive insurance benefits, and proceed with other estate-related procedures. New Jersey law also allows declaration of death where a person has gone missing after a catastrophe — a flood or hurricane, for example — as publicly recognized by the state governor, in which case, time of death is presumed to be the time of the occurrence of the catastrophe.

The advantage of probate court is that if you have a feuding family or just do not care what happens to your belongings when you are gone, the state laws, through the court, will take care of it for you. If either case is true, then you can save yourself the work of the annual review process. If you prefer to direct things yourself, the annual review process can prevent extensive probate involvement.

If you name a beneficiary for a trust or insurance policy and that person declines the bequest or predeceases you, the secondary beneficiary will inherit. If you do not have a secondary beneficiary named, then the probate court will settle the matter because your estate becomes the beneficiary. Any issues that you do not account for in your will, will alternatives, or other estate-distribution activities will be settled by the probate court because property must not remain in limbo.

Taking a few hours each year to make sure your documents are in place and up-to-date is a small investment compared to the effort and angst otherwise shifted to those who survive you.

Identity Theft

As you collect information about all your assets and liabilities and compile important personal information, it is important to be aware of safeguarding the related documentation. Identify theft is a quite real, dangerous threat. A person representing himself or herself as another individual is a crime that can be prevented. When you do not think like a criminal, it can be difficult to figure out what you need to do to protect yourself.

Some of the ways in which a skilled identity thief will steal your information might surprise you. The following are ways to consider:

- **Change of address:** By submitting a change-of-address card with the U.S. Postal Service (USPS), the thief will send your mail to a location where he or she can get at it without suspicion.

- **Stealing:** Taking mail out of your mailbox is a bit more risky, but it does happen. Completing and returning pre-approved credit cards with a change of address is just one way your mail can be used to steal your identity (along with stealing your wallet, taking personal records from an employer, or offering bribes to employees who have access to sell your information).

- **Garbage diving:** This is the act of looking through trash to find bills or bank statements with account information or any personal information that might be useful in the act of stealing someone's identity, such as a social security number, mother's maiden name, or personal identification number (PIN). This is not considered theft; the U.S. Supreme Court has ruled that anything left out for trash collection is in the public domain.

- **Skimming:** This is accomplished by using a special high-tech storage device that electronically "grabs" your account number and other personal information when a store computer is processing your credit card purchase/transaction.

- **Phishing:** A thief will pretend to represent a bank, some other financial institution, or a legitimate business in the form of an e-mail or as a pop-up communication when you visit a website.

These communications will ask you to verify or correct information provided and then ask for additional personal information.

Avoiding identity theft

If you want to avoid being robbed on the street, there are some common-sense things you can do without going to a "How Not to Get Mugged" class. Do not walk alone in a strange neighborhood at night, and only park in brightly lit parking lots. Like these behaviors, there are some obvious things people do that help prevent identify theft, such as cutting up old credit cards instead of throwing them into the trash intact. But if you throw all the pieces into the same garbage bag, a thief can reassemble the pieces and make Internet purchases because the thief will have access to the security code on the back of the card.

Through the unfortunate experiences of those who have had their credit rating destroyed, among other unfortunate consequences, the methods of identity thieves are no longer a secret. There are many things you can do to avoid being robbed of your good name.

The first and most important thing is awareness: Pay attention to what you are doing with your personal information. If you are scribbling notes about the accounts you need to look up and then jot them down on a piece of paper so that you can enter them into a spreadsheet, do not throw that paper into the trash. Create a pile or special trash can for "personal info." Put anything that needs to be disposed of in that one place, such as old utility bills, bank statements from an account you closed ten years ago, or statements from your insurance company telling you that a reimbursement has been made to your primary-care physician. Then choose a method for making those documents unreadable.

Invest in a small, crosscut shredder — because larger scraps of paper can be reassembled like a puzzle. Remember the news clips of federal investigators hauling out bags of shredded documents from a national corporation under investigation? If your documents are not old and dusty, call your local animal shelter and ask whether they can use shredded paper for litter boxes. It is not very likely a thief is going to want to go through that much effort to go through your documents once the cats, dogs, or guinea pigs are done with them. Most shredders will also destroy credit cards — make sure you do not mix your plastic with paper going to the shelter. If you want to be supersafe with your credit card bits, separate the plastic bits into several different trash cans and dispose of them at different times.

Burning paper until it is a powdery ash also works well. Some other ways to prevent identity theft are equally simple, after you have them in mind.

- Never give out personal information to a stranger over the telephone or via blind mailers. If you want to register an appliance or request more information from a company, call it. Do not fill out a postcard that asks for your e-mail address, birth date, or other personal data that can be read and copied by anyone who sees it.

- Treat your social security number like gold; guard it the same way you would a gold coin. Do not carry your social security card in your wallet or purse, and never write it on a check. Only provide it when absolutely necessary, and then only to someone you have verified as an authorized agent for the company with whom you share it.

- Passwords for any account need to be unusual — do not use the birth dates of your children, your wedding anniversary, any portion of your social security number, or your telephone number. Some of that information is easy to obtain through public records requests, and it will provide open access to your accounts.

- Never communicate personal information via e-mail. If you need to get the information to someone quickly, call and leave a message in a private voice-mail box or send a fax to a confidential location where the information will not be handled by many people. If e-mail is a necessary means for communicating, never send complete information in one e-mail: send most of your social security number in one e-mail, and send the last four digits in a second e-mail. Same with account numbers — even better is to e-mail part and call with the remainder. Electronic communications should not be considered secure — they can be intercepted or read by someone other than your intended audience.

- If a delivery person says he or she is with the U.S. Postal Service (USPS) but is stopping by to drop off a package for a friend on her way home after changing out of uniform, refuse the package and tell this person that your usual letter carrier can come back tomorrow in uniform, and you will sign for it then. If this feels like being paranoid and untrusting, that is all right. You would not give your child to a stranger, so do not give yourself either in the form of your personal information.

Be on the lookout

First and foremost, this means to protect any official documents or written materials — such as the completed worksheets from this book — so that nobody has access to them unless you grant them permission. A locking file cabinet with a limited number of keys that are not numbered is one option. Standard file cabinets, like the ones you can get from large manufacturers, have a number written on the lock. If you lose the key, you can give them that number and a few dollars, and they will send a replacement — but they will do the same for a thief, no questions asked.

A fire-resistant safe or lockbox that you can store at home also will work. These safes are not fireproof, meaning whatever is inside will not necessarily survive in any fire. Fire-resistant means what is inside will be protected for a number of hours before the safe itself gets so hot that flammable material will catch fire and disintegrate. Portable boxes also can be stolen. None of this means you should not bother with these options; it just means you should be aware of the limitations of your choices.

Other choices you have for protection are being on the lookout for unusual problems:

- You are denied credit when you think your credit rating is sound.

- Bills or other information, such as letters or warranty offers, arrive for purchases you did not make.

- Bills that come at the same time every month or related to a specific purchase do not arrive as anticipated.

- Credit cards or account statements for which you did not apply are delivered.

If any of these events happen, investigate. Along those same lines, request a copy of your credit report on a regular basis, at least once a year, and check it for unusual activity; immediately follow up on anything that is suspicious. Federal law now requires nationwide credit reporting agencies to provide one free copy of your credit report each year, upon request. Visit www.annualcreditreport.com or call 1-877-322-8228 and request your free report. You can also write to:

Annual Credit Report Request Service
PO Box 105281
Atlanta, GA 30348-5281

Review any statements you get about existing accounts — credit card, checking, savings, money market — and see whether anything is out of place. If something is wrong or some vital information has been stolen, act immediately.

Close any accounts that have been set up in your name but not by your doing, or any account of yours that has been meddled with. Report the trouble immediately to your local police by filing a police report. Prepare an ID Theft Affidavit with the Federal Trade Commission, available via www.ftc.gov or report it via telephone at 1-877-ID-THEFT (438-4338) or TTY 1-866-653-4261. Traditional mail is also an option:

Identity Theft Clearinghouse
Federal Trade Commission
Washington. D.C. 20580

You also can place a fraud alert on your credit report; this instructs creditors to follow specific procedures before a new account is opened in your name. They also will follow these procedures when a change of personal information is requested. Before any action is taken, you can receive a phone call that will require the verification of a combination of specific personal information that would be difficult for a thief to have all at one time. There are only a few national credit reporting companies, so calling one company will let the others know that an alert has been requested — no need for you to call all three.

Equifax: 1-800-525-6285   **TransUnion:** 1-800-680-7289
Experian: 1-800-397-3742

Identity theft is a threat that should be taken seriously. Educate yourself and your family, and you will reduce your chances of being victimized.

Additional resources:
- About identity theft:
  - Federal Trade Commission: **www.ftc.gov/idtheft**
  - Identity Theft Resource Center: **www.idtheftcenter.org**
  - Social Security Administration: **www.socialsecurity.gov/pubs/10064.pdf**
- For victims of identity theft:
  - Privacy Rights Clearinghouse: **www.privacyrights.org**
  - Office of Justice Programs, Office for Victims of Crimes (OVC): **www.ojp.usdoj.gov/ovc/help/it.htm**

CONCLUSION

Congratulations: You have an estate to plan. It turns out you do not have to be rich, famous, or pompous to have the kind of resources that make it necessary to plan for the future.

The single most important thing you can do now is to create an estate plan. Even if you have done all the exercises in this book, you know there is much more work to do. The work that is necessary to move from where you are now to the point where you are scheduling regular annual meetings with estate professionals might seem a monumental task. But the good news is that it can be done. You have enough information to ask informed questions and begin to narrow down this huge idea of estate planning into your goals, will, and trusts.

The need to create your own definitions is why you did not find sample wills, a standard trust document, or an annuity template in these pages; it is counterproductive. Trying to shoehorn your information into a pre-scribed form supports a cookie-cutter approach to something that is highly personal — you are the one who loses with that kind of approach. The things you want to accomplish with the results of your years of hard work are not going to be like those of your brother Ben or your sister Sally. There will always be similarities, which is why books like this exist, but they need to serve as a place to begin, not end.

Customization takes time and stirs up considerable emotion — maybe even issues you would rather not face. Take your time and get the help you need with all of it. If you set your own pace and find people with whom you are comfortable, you will avoid unnecessary frustration, upset, and expense.

This is a big commitment, but when compared to the commitments it took to get to the point where you need to consider estate planning, this is a manageable process.

Build in some fun to get yourself through the difficult things. Every time you reach a milestone, like completing your will, treat yourself to a dinner out or spend a day lounging under a tree reading a book. Always remind yourself of the gifts you give that cannot be delineated in writing — your wish to make your departure less burdensome, your thoughtfulness, and your love for the people in your life — which are all communicated through the effort of this work.

Jersey City Skylines by the Hudson River

APPENDIX A

Estate-Planning Worksheets

Your Estate in Black and White

Page 1

Name _____ Birth _____ SS# _____

Spouse _____ Birth _____ SS# _____

Primary Address _____ # of Minors _____

Child _____ Birth _____ SS# _____

Child _____ Birth _____ SS# _____

Guardian of _____ Birth _____ SS# _____

ASSETS				
Real Estate: *primary residence, vacation home, land*				
Address/ Description	Ownership	Mortgage(s)	Purchase Price/Year	**Current Value**
Automobile(s)				
Year	Make	Model	Ownership	**Current Value**
Accounts: *checking, savings, certificate of deposit, brokerage*				
Type	Beneficiary(ies)		Account #	**Current Value**
Life Insurance				
Company	Insured	Beneficiary(ies)	Ownership	Face Value	**Current Value**
Retirement: *401(k), IRA, Roth IRA, Keogh, pension, profit sharing, social security*				
Plan	Ownership **Current Value**	Beneficiary(ies)		**Vested Year/ Percent**
Other Financial Assets: *stocks, bonds, inheritance, structured settlement, rent payments*				
Type	Beneficiary(ies)	Ownership		**Current Value**
Personal Property: *boat/jet ski, jewelry, artwork, antiques, collectibles, household contents, etc.*				
Type	Value	Purchase Year		**Current Value**

Page 2

ADDITIONAL ASSETS			
List all the things that did not fit on the preceding page of the inventory sheet:			
Type	Value	Purchase Year	**Current Value**

$ _____

Total Assets $ _____

LIABILITIES			
First mortgage, second mortgage, line of credit, car loan, and credit card balance, for example:			
Type	Ownership	Due/Payoff Year	**Current Value**

Total Liabilities $ _____

Total Assets $ _____

Total Liabilities $ _____

Total Net Worth   = $ _____

Prioritization

This is about making choices regarding what you can and cannot do with your estate. Indicate your six key values. These are the values or qualities to which you are attracted:

1.	
2.	
3.	
4.	
5.	
6.	

Then, add the one key value to orient your life around: _____

_____

Now list all of the things you would like to accomplish with your estate planning, and connect those with your highest values: If more than one value is accomplished, note that.

		Goals	Value
1.	$5k	*Leave a substantial amount of money to cat shelter*	*Involvement*
2.	$50k	*Education funds for nieces and nephews*	*Education*
3.	$		
4.	$		
5.	$		
6.	$		
7.	$		
8.	$		
9.	$		
10.	$		
11.	$		

After you have completed your list of goals, place an approximate dollar value for the gift you would like to leave in the left-hand margin. Use a range if you are not sure.

Total Gifts $ _____

Who, What, How, and When

After you decide on the people and organizations to receive bequests, take a moment to write out your list. This will be useful when you sit down with your estate-planning team to finalize the paperwork and implementation of your estate plan. Leave any places blank if you are unsure.

Who/ relationship	What	How	When	Special Circumstances
Jeanine/niece	*$50,000 + books ($10k value)*	*Trust (bequest)*	*2011*	*Will*
Cat shelter/charity	*$5,000*	*Bequest*	*2011*	*Will*
Danny/brother	*$250,000*	*Living trust/bequest*	*2011*	*Will*

Essential Documents and Accounts Inventory

Life will go on after you die, and handling your estate will likely fall to people who are mired in grief. To make it easier to find and deal with the accounts and obligations you leave behind, consolidate as much information as possible. This worksheet is a place to begin compiling this data.

This information will also be helpful to have when you meet with your estate planner.

DEBTS
Mortgage
Company Name:
Account Number:
Contact:
Phone Number:
E-Mail Address:
Payment Amount:
Usual Due Date:
Method of Payment: *(automatic deductions for checking / savings, online bill payment via bank, coupon with check)*
PIN: *(Personal identification number)*
Secret Question:
Answer:
Second Mortgage
Company Name:
Account Number:
Contact:
Phone Number:
E-Mail Address:
Payment Amount:
Usual Due Date:
Method of Payment:
PIN:

Secret Question:	
Answer:	
Timeshare — Mortgage Information	
Company Name:	
Account Number:	
Contact:	
Phone Number:	
E-Mail Address:	
Payment Amount:	
Usual Due Date:	
Method of Payment:	
PIN:	
Secret Question:	
Answer:	
Vacation Property — Mortgage Information	
Company Name:	
Account Number:	
Contact:	
Phone Number:	
E-Mail Address:	
Payment Amount:	
Usual Due Date:	
Method of Payment:	
PIN:	
Secret Question:	
Answer:	
Loans — Home Equity	
Company Name:	
Account Number:	
Contact:	
Phone Number:	
E-Mail Address:	
Payment Amount:	
Usual Due Date:	
Method of Payment:	
PIN:	
Secret Question:	
Answer:	

Loans — Line of Credit	
Company Name:	
Account Number:	
Contact:	
Phone Number:	
E-Mail Address:	
Payment Amount:	
Usual Due Date:	
Method of Payment:	
PIN:	
Secret Question:	
Answer:	
Loans — Signature	
Company Name:	
Account Number:	
Contact:	
Phone Number:	
E-Mail Address:	
Payment Amount:	
Usual Due Date:	
Method of Payment:	
PIN:	
Secret Question:	
Answer:	
Loans — Student / College Tuition	
Company Name:	
Account Number:	
Contact:	
Phone Number:	
E-Mail Address:	
Payment Amount:	
Usual Due Date:	
Method of Payment:	
PIN:	
Secret Question:	
Answer:	

Loans — Automobile
Company Name:
Account Number:
Contact:
Phone Number:
E-Mail Address:
Payment Amount:
Usual Due Date:
Method of Payment:
PIN:
Secret Question:
Answer:
Loans — Other (boat, second car, etc.)
Company Name:
Account Number:
Contact:
Phone Number:
E-Mail Address:
Payment Amount:
Usual Due Date:
Method of Payment:
PIN:
Secret Question:
Answer:
Credit Card 1
Company Name:
Account Number:
Contact:
Phone Number:
E-Mail Address:
Payment Amount:
Usual Due Date:
Method of Payment:
PIN:
Secret Question:
Answer:

Credit Card 2
Company Name:
Account Number:
Contact:
Phone Number:
E-Mail Address:
Payment Amount:
Usual Due Date:
Method of Payment:
PIN:
Secret Question:
Answer:
Credit Card 3
Company Name:
Account Number:
Contact:
Phone Number:
E-Mail Address:
Payment Amount:
Usual Due Date:
Method of Payment:
PIN:
Secret Question:
Answer:
Other — Account 1
Company Name:
Account Number:
Contact:
Phone Number:
E-Mail Address:
Payment Amount:
Usual Due Date:
Method of Payment:
PIN:
Secret Question:
Answer:

Other — Account 2
Company Name:
Account Number:
Contact:
Phone Number:
E-Mail Address:
Payment Amount:
Usual Due Date:
Method of Payment:
PIN:
Secret Question:
Answer:

Other — Account 3
Company Name:
Account Number:
Contact:
Phone Number:
E-Mail Address:
Payment Amount:
Usual Due Date:
Method of Payment:
PIN:
Secret Question:
Answer:

LIVING EXPENSES

Gas and Electric
Company Name:
Account Number:
Contact:
Phone Number:
E-Mail Address:
Payment Amount:
Usual Due Date:
Method of Payment:
PIN:
Secret Question:
Answer:

Water and Sewer (or septic)	
Company Name:	
Account Number:	
Contact:	
Phone Number:	
E-Mail Address:	
Payment Amount:	
Usual Due Date:	
Method of Payment:	
PIN:	
Secret Question:	
Answer:	
Telephone	
Company Name:	
Account Number:	
Contact:	
Phone Number:	
E-Mail Address:	
Payment Amount:	
Usual Due Date:	
Method of Payment:	
PIN:	
Secret Question:	
Answer:	
Heating Oil	
Company Name:	
Account Number:	
Contact:	
Phone Number:	
E-Mail Address:	
Payment Amount:	
Usual Due Date:	
Method of Payment:	
PIN:	
Secret Question:	
Answer:	
Internet Service Provider (ISP)	
Company Name:	

Account Number:	
Contact:	
Phone Number:	
E-Mail Address:	
Payment Amount:	
Usual Due Date:	
Method of Payment:	
PIN:	
Secret Question:	
Answer:	
Cable / Satellite Television Service	
Company Name:	
Account Number:	
Contact:	
Phone Number:	
E-Mail Address:	
Payment Amount:	
Usual Due Date:	
Method of Payment:	
PIN:	
Secret Question:	
Answer:	
Other — Account 1	
Company Name:	
Account Number:	
Contact:	
Phone Number:	
E-Mail Address:	
Payment Amount:	
Usual Due Date:	
Method of Payment:	
PIN:	
Secret Question:	
Answer:	
Other — Account 2	
Company Name:	
Account Number:	
Contact:	

Phone Number:	
E-Mail Address:	
Payment Amount:	
Usual Due Date:	
Method of Payment:	
PIN:	
Secret Question:	
Answer:	

OTHER REGULAR PAYMENTS

Insurance: Life — Policy 1

Company Name:	
Account Number:	
Contact:	
Phone Number:	
E-Mail Address:	
Payment Amount:	
Usual Due Date:	
Method of Payment:	
PIN:	
Secret Question:	
Answer:	

Insurance: Life — Policy 2

Company Name:	
Account Number:	
Contact:	
Phone Number:	
E-Mail Address:	
Payment Amount:	
Usual Due Date:	
Method of Payment:	
PIN:	
Secret Question:	
Answer:	

Insurance: Life — Disability (Long-/Short-Term)

Company Name:	
Account Number:	
Contact:	
Phone Number:	

E-Mail Address:	
Payment Amount:	
Usual Due Date:	
Method of Payment:	
PIN:	
Secret Question:	
Answer:	
Insurance: Life — Homeowner's / Renter's	
Company Name:	
Account Number:	
Contact:	
Phone Number:	
E-Mail Address:	
Payment Amount:	
Usual Due Date:	
Method of Payment:	
PIN:	
Secret Question:	
Answer:	
Insurance: Car — Policy 1	
Company Name:	
Account Number:	
Contact:	
Phone Number:	
E-Mail Address:	
Payment Amount:	
Usual Due Date:	
Method of Payment:	
PIN:	
Secret Question:	
Answer:	
Insurance: Car — Policy 2	
Company Name:	
Account Number:	
Contact:	
Phone Number:	
E-Mail Address:	
Payment Amount:	

Usual Due Date:	
Method of Payment:	
PIN:	
Secret Question:	
Answer:	
Newspaper Subscription 1	
Company Name:	
Account Number:	
Contact:	
Phone Number:	
E-Mail Address:	
Payment Amount:	
Usual Due Date:	
Method of Payment:	
Newspaper Subscription 2	
Company Name:	
Account Number:	
Contact:	
Phone Number:	
E-Mail Address:	
Payment Amount:	
Usual Due Date:	
Method of Payment:	
Magazine Subscription 1	
Company Name:	
Account Number:	
Contact:	
Phone Number:	
E-Mail Address:	
Payment Amount:	
Usual Due Date:	
Method of Payment:	
Magazine Subscription 2	
Company Name:	
Account Number:	
Contact:	
Phone Number:	

E-Mail Address:	
Payment Amount:	
Usual Due Date:	
Method of Payment:	
Magazine Subscription 3	
Company Name:	
Account Number:	
Contact:	
Phone Number:	
E-Mail Address:	
Payment Amount:	
Usual Due Date:	
Method of Payment:	
Other — Account 1	
Company Name:	
Account Number:	
Contact:	
Phone Number:	
E-Mail Address:	
Payment Amount:	
Usual Due Date:	
Method of Payment:	
PIN:	
Secret Question:	
Answer:	
Other — Account 2	
Company Name:	
Account Number:	
Contact:	
Phone Number:	
E-Mail Address:	
Payment Amount:	
Usual Due Date:	
Method of Payment:	
PIN:	
Secret Question:	
Answer:	

INCOME

Payroll Check 1
Company Name:
Account Number:
Contact:
Phone Number:
E-Mail Address:
Check Amount:
Pay Day/Dates:
Method of Payment: *(check, direct deposit, cash, other)*
Additional Important Information:

Payroll Check 2
Company Name:
Account Number:
Contact:
Phone Number:
E-Mail Address:
Check Amount:
Pay Day/Dates:
Method of Payment: *(check, direct deposit, cash, other)*
Additional Important Information:

Structured Settlement
Company Name:
Account Number:
Contact:
Phone Number:
E-Mail Address:
Check Amount:
Day/Dates Paid:
Method of Payment: *(check, direct deposit, cash, other)*
Additional Important Information:

Royalty Payment 1
Company Name:
Account Number:
Contact:
Phone Number:
E-Mail Address:
Check Amount:
Day/Dates Paid:
Method of Payment: *(check, direct deposit, cash, other)*
Additional Important Information:

Royalty Payment 2
Company Name:
Account Number:
Contact:
Phone Number:
E-Mail Address:
Check Amount:
Day/Dates Paid:
Method of Payment: *(check, direct deposit, cash, other)*
Additional Important Information:

Annuity Payment 1
Company Name:
Account Number:
Contact:
Phone Number:
E-Mail Address:
Check Amount:
Day/Dates Paid:
Method of Payment: *(check, direct deposit, cash, other)*
Additional Important Information:

Annuity Payment 2
Company Name:
Account Number:
Contact:
Phone Number:
E-Mail Address:
Check Amount:
Day/Dates Paid:
Method of Payment: *(check, direct deposit, cash, other)*
Additional Important Information:

Retirement Distribution — Plan 1
Company Name:
Account Number:
Contact:
Phone Number:
E-Mail Address:
Check Amount:
Day/Dates Paid:
Method of Payment: *(check, direct deposit, cash, other)*
Additional Important Information:

Retirement Distribution — Plan 2
Company Name:
Account Number:
Contact:
Phone Number:
E-Mail Address:
Check Amount:
Day/Dates Paid:
Method of Payment: *(check, direct deposit, cash, other)*

Rental Property 1
Company Name:
Account Number:
Contact:

Phone Number:	
E-Mail Address:	
Check Amount:	
Day/Dates Paid:	
Method of Payment: *(check, direct deposit, cash, other)*	
Tenant Information:	

Rental Property 2

Company Name:	
Account Number:	
Contact:	
Phone Number:	
E-Mail Address:	
Check Amount:	
Day/Dates Paid:	
Method of Payment: *(check, direct deposit, cash, other)*	
Tenant Information:	

FINANCIAL RESOURCES

Checking — Account 1

Financial Institution:	
Account Number:	
Contact:	
Phone Number:	
E-Mail Address:	
Balance:	
Date:	
PIN:	
Secret Question:	
Answer:	
Additional Important Information:	

Checking — Account 2

Financial Institution:	
Account Number:	
Contact:	

Phone Number:	
E-Mail Address:	
Balance:	
Date:	
PIN:	
Secret Question:	
Answer:	
Additional Important Information:	
Savings — Account 1	
Financial Institution:	
Account Number:	
Contact:	
Phone Number:	
E-Mail Address:	
Balance:	
Date:	
PIN:	
Secret Question:	
Answer:	
Additional Important Information:	
Savings — Account 2	
Financial Institution;	
Account Number:	
Contact:	
Phone Number:	
E-Mail Address:	
Balance:	
Date:	
PIN:	
Secret Question:	
Answer:	
Additional Important Information:	
Certificate of Deposit — Account 1	

Financial Institution:
Account Number:
Contact:
Phone Number:
E-Mail Address:
Balance:
Date:
PIN:
Secret Question:
Answer:
Additional Important Information:

Certificate of Deposit — Account 2
Financial Institution:
Account Number:
Contact:
Phone Number:
E-Mail Address:
Balance:
Date:
PIN:
Secret Question:
Answer:
Additional Important Information:

Money Market Fund — Account 1
Financial Institution:
Account Number:
Contact:
Phone Number:
E-Mail Address:
Balance:
Date:
PIN:
Secret Question:
Answer:

Additional Important Information:

Money Market Fund — Account 2
Financial Institution:
Account Number:
Contact:
Phone Number:
E-Mail Address:
Balance:
Date:
PIN:
Secret Question:
Answer:
Additional Important Information:

Other — Account 1
Financial Institution:
Account Number:
Contact:
Phone Number:
E-Mail Address:
Balance:
Date:
PIN:
Secret Question:
Answer:
Additional Important Information:

Other — Account 2
Financial Institution:
Account Number:
Contact:
Phone Number:
E-Mail Address:
Balance:
Date:
PIN:

Secret Question:
Answer:
Additional Important Information:

Anything that did not fit in a predetermined category: _____

_____

_____

_____

Party Planning with an Unusual Twist

Whether you prefer a traditional and dignified ceremony, or an occasion that is a reflection of how you lived your life, the arrangements for the last event you will attend on Earth in this lifetime can be up to you. But you need to make the necessary arrangements, or direct others to do as you wish. *This is not a legally binding document; a lawyer will need to be consulted for the correct language and paperwork.*

Check all that apply (leave blank those things you do not want) and provide any details that are needed.

Your body:

☐ I want my body to be donated to medicine and used for the following purposes: _____

_____

☐ Release the final report, including all test results, to my executor/ personal representative: _____

_____

☐ Conduct a post-mortem examination if the following circumstances occur: _____

_____

☐ Cremate my remains, and disposal of my ashes should be conducted as follows: _____

_____

☐ I request a burial to take place in this way: _____

_____

Your service:

☐ I want a memorial service without a casket.

☐ I want a funeral without a casket.

☐ Memorial service with a casket conducted in the following manner:

☐ Closed
☐ Open
☐ Funeral home/mortuary: _____
Address: _____
Phone: _____

☐ I would like a funeral service conducted in the following manner:

Place of worship: _____

Address: _____

Phone: _____

Presiding clergy: _____

Soloist: _____

Hymns: _____

_____

Musical selections: _____

_____

Musical instruments: _____

_____

Scripture, poem(s), and other materials to be included: _____

_____

_____

Other instructions: _____

_____

_____

_____

_____

Memorial gifts should be suggested for the following: _____

_____

_____

Other information: _____

_____

_____

Signed: _____ Date: _____

Estate-Plan Summary Sheet

Many components can go into an estate plan, but there are basic documents that most people have. This is a brief inventory that can serve as a checklist for making sure you get the things done that you need to accomplish.

Use the blank lines to add other documents, such as a prenuptial agreement, that will affect your estate plan.

Estate Plan Components	Deadline	Done On	Notes
Estate Plan Summary Sheet			
Will			
Living Will			
Organ Donor Form/Card			
Durable Power of Attorney			
Medical Power of Attorney			
Guardians for Children			
Guardians for Others			
Life Insurance Policies			
Trust: For Children			
Trust: For Retirement			
Trust: For Charity _____			
Trust: For Charity _____			
Trust: Living _____			
Retirement: 401(k)/Pension _____ _____ _____ _____			

Use the Notes sections as reminders for additional information that is needed before the next review; for example, "Get name of Peace Center lawyer" to make sure you have a contact for the charitable trust documents that might need to get to this organization.

Annual To-Do List

Once your estate plan is complete, this list will need to be customized to include each component.

Use the blank lines to add other documents, such as a prenuptial agreement, that will affect your estate plan.

Estate Plan Pieces	Meeting Date	Changes Needed
Estate Plan Summary Sheet		
Will		
Living Will		
Organ Donor Form/Card		
Durable Power of Attorney		
Medical Power of Attorney		
Guardians for Children		
Guardians for Others		
Life Insurance Policies		
Trust: _____		
Trust: _____		
Trust: _____		
Trust: _____		
Retirement: _____		

Retirement: _____
_____
_____
_____
_____

Notes:

APPENDIX B

Glossary of Terms

401(k) Plan – Named after the IRS code number defining this kind of plan, this retirement savings plan allows contributions to be made automatically by your employer via deductions from your paycheck, pre-tax. This plan only applies to for-profit businesses.

403(b) Plan – This is the 401(k) equivalent for not-for-profit entities and is named after the IRS code number defining this kind of retirement savings plan. It allows contributions to be made automatically by your employer via deductions from your paycheck, pre-tax.

A

Adeemed – The status given to a will if property is missing from your estate that is specifically named in the will.

Ademption Statute – State law governing the distribution of property in an estate if items are missing or adeemed.

Administrator – If you die without a will, the court appoints an individual, normally a spouse or child, who will serve in the same capacity as an executor. That person will handle all the estate paperwork, prepare a list of assets, deal with likely heirs, handle claims from creditors, make payments on outstanding debt, and handle other estate-related matters.

Annuity – A retirement investment account you create by contributing a specific amount of money over a predetermined period of time; there will be a fixed rate of return for a number of years.

▶ **Variable Annuity** – A retirement investment account you create by contributing a specific amount of money over a predetermined period of time; the funds are invested in the stock market, so the return depends on how well or poorly the economy does.

Antilapse – The status of a will if a beneficiary in your will dies before you do.

Antilapse Statute – State law that dictates the state will intervene if the property in a will exists, but the beneficiary is no longer alive and no contingent beneficiary is named.

Appointment Clause – A giving clause in your will that identifies the person who will manage your estate.

Asset – Anything a person owns or is owed; this can be money, real estate, investments, or any other tangible property.

Automobile Insurance – The exchange of premiums for a guaranteed payment to cover the damage or loss of a motor vehicle. Medical and liability coverage also can be included.

B

Bargain Sale – The sale of a piece of property to a charity at a rate that is below the fair market value. The difference between the amount paid and actual value is the amount of the gift.

Beneficiary – The individual(s) or group(s) that will receive the property in a will or trust. This can be a single person (a nephew), a group of people (all grandchildren), one group (Stray Cat Rescue, Inc.), several groups (all community councils in your city), or a combination of any of these.

Beneficial Title, or Equitable Title – The right of a person or institution to take possession of or benefit from the property in a trust.

Bequest – A legacy or gift given by a person to another person or entity through a last will and testament after the giver dies.

Burial Trust – Provides the funds necessary to cover the cost of your burial (or cremation) arrangements; this can be a revocable trust, but after your death it becomes irrevocable, and the trust cannot be used for anything else.

Bypass Trust – This trust will transfer property to someone other than your spouse, such as a child or grandchild, but will allow him or her to still benefit from the property in the trust.

C

Certified Public Accountant (CPA) – A person who has gone through professional training and meets state requirements for both education and work experience, passed a national accounting exam, and met other licensing requirements to perform the tasks of accounting, such as performing audits, preparing tax returns, and giving advice to clients — individuals or businesses — on financial matters. Accountants can also specialize in various aspects of financial estate matters, such as trusts, annuities, and estate tax law. But they also serve as estate-planning specialists who can help you consider all financial decisions.

Charitable Trust – A method for giving charitable institutions gifts, including regular support on a time-release basis, that are tax-free for the donor.

Charitable Remainder Trust – Gives gifts of interest income that are paid to specific beneficiaries, such as a charity or a spouse, for a specific period of time; at the end of that time period, the charity receives whatever is left in the trust.

Charitable Lead Trust – Also known as a front trust; gives the charity a specific gift before all other beneficiaries receive anything.

Clauses – The sections in your will that organize information in a specific order.

Coach – These trained professionals specialize in offering financial, professional, and personal guidance to help you identify and manage monetary, career, and personal goals. There are certification courses for various forms of coaching, but there are no national standards, and formal training is not required to present oneself as a coach.

Codicil – A separate legal document that adds provisions to an existing will.

Cost-of-living Adjustment – Some plans have a variable that allows for annual increases in the payments made to the employee to help cover the cost of rising prices. Not all plans have this feature.

Crummey Trust – An extremely complicated trust normally set up in conjunction with an irrevocable life insurance trust to make the payments for a life insurance policy; this is a type of trust that requires an estate-planning attorney.

Custodian Account – This account for minor children, which can be in the form of a trust, allows you to deposit money or property in an account set up by a bank or brokerage firm. You can name yourself as the custodian, or trustee, of the account while you are alive and then name a successor to take over those responsibilities after your death.

► **Uniform Transfer to Minors Act (UTMA)** – This is the most current federal regulation that defines and allows an account, or trust, to be set up for minor children; if a state adopted this regulation, it served to repeal their UGMA statute. UTMA is the law followed in New Jersey where UTMA trusts remain in place until the child reaches age 21.

► **Uniform Gift to Minors Act (UGMA)** – This is the first federal regulation that defined and allows an account, or trust, to be set up for minor children; some states still have this form of the law on their books, but if they have also enacted UTMA, the latter supersedes UGMA.

D

Decedent – A person who has died.

Disability Insurance – A disability insurance policy that will make payments to you to cover living expenses and replace your lost income as a result of your inability to hold a job.

▶ **Short-term Disability** – Provides benefits for about three months; some plans go a little longer, but only for a short period of time.

▶ **Long-term Disability** – Provides benefits for years but does eventually end, frequently at age 65, when you become eligible for social security.

Disclaimer – A refusal of a beneficiary to accept the gift given; recognized by both federal and state authorities if given in writing by a specific deadline, typically nine months after the donor's death.

Discretionary Trust – Gives a trustee the ability to distribute income and property to a variety of beneficiaries; he or she also has the option to control the distributions to a single beneficiary as he or she decides is appropriate.

Distribution – This is the disbursement or payment of property from an account to a beneficiary; it could be in the form of a check or some other monetary payment, or the transfer of a title into the name of the beneficiary.

Distribution Provisions – Any clause that identifies to whom the income will be given and the frequency of those distributions, such as payments made every April 15 to the IRS.

DNR – Do not resuscitate: an advanced medical directive that expresses your wish to not be resuscitated or revived if you appear to have died.

Donee – The person or institution receiving a gift.

Donor – The person who gives a gift or bequest.

Dumpster Diving – A slang term used to describe the act of digging through trash to find bills, bank statements, or other documents with account information or any personal information that might be useful to an identity thief; this is not considered an act of theft because the U.S. Supreme Court ruled that anything left out for trash collection is in the public domain.

Durable Power of Attorney – Allows an authorized person to act on behalf of the grantor of that power of attorney.

Dynasty Trust – Also known as a wealth trust; can last for several generations or be set up to never end. This kind of trust helps people with a vast amount of wealth control the distribution of that money and property over a long period of time.

E

Educational Trust – This is a kind of protective trust that sets aside money specifically for education-related expenses, such as tuition or training fees, books, or supplies. These trusts include provisions to stop payments if the student drops out of school or flunks numerous classes.

Ending Clauses – These include the legalities to meet statutory requirements so that your will is legal and valid, which include (but are not limited to) your signature, date and location of the signing, and witnesses.

Estate Planning – Creating a set of instructions about what should be done with your things — money, possessions, investments, collectibles, or anything you own — before and after you die.

Estate Tax – Referred to as the "death tax" by Congress, this is the federal tax on the property in your estate after you die.

Executor – Also called a personal representative, this is the individual who handles the property you leave behind. If you die without a will, the court appoints an administrator, frequently a spouse or child.

Exemption – This is a specific amount of money that will not be affected by estate taxes. Federal taxes and states with an estate tax often set an amount, such as $1 million, that is tax-free, then taxes are due on $1.01 million and beyond.

F

Family Consent – Also known as a health surrogate, this is a family member designated by state law who will make medical decisions for you when you cannot do it for yourself. These laws follow a specific order of kinship for who makes a decision — if you are married, your spouse, not your sister, will be your surrogate.

Family Trust – A legal arrangement that involves the transfer of property from the original owner to a family member for the purpose of holding and maintaining the property until the beneficiary takes ownership.

Fiduciary Powers Clause – A giving clause in your will that includes language giving your executor the power to serve as your executor, including any duties that go beyond the basic requirements in your state regulations.

Financial Planner – Certified Financial Planners® (CFP®), Chartered Financial Analysts (CFA), and other planners without these titles are individuals who analyze the overall financial situation of an individual and then develop a comprehensive plan, in conjunction with the individual, that will attempt to meet his or her financial goals and objectives. Planners who are certified have followed a specific course of education or training classes, and some go on to develop expertise in specific areas, such as estate or retirement planning.

Funding a Trust – The placement of property in a trust; that same property will be called "trust principal" once it is under the auspices of the trust agreement.

G

Generation-Skipping Tax Transfer (GSTT) – This is a federal tax levied on property transferred to a person one or more generations removed from the donor.

Generation-Skipping Transfer Trust – A tax-saving trust that is designed to benefit multiple generations after you are gone.

Gift Tax – A federal tax levied against any property you give to another person or institution during a fiscal year; it can be in cash or the transfer of property, such as real estate or jewelry.

Giving Clauses – Explain what property goes to which person and under what circumstances. These causes can be as broad or explicit as you want. Real property clauses are statements that match up property with a person. Personal property clauses are used when you want to be explicit in your instructions. A residuary clause addresses the "leftovers" in your estate that you do not single out in a clause; this clause is essential for any kind of will to make sure that anything you forget or acquire since the will was prepared can be distributed. Assigning one or two beneficiaries is a good idea to keep your assets out of the hands of the courts.

Grantor-Retained Trusts – These are irrevocable, noncharitable trusts, which means they are set up in a way that is similar to a charitable trust, but the beneficiary is not a charity. There are three common types:

▶ **GRAT** – Grantor-retained annuity trust gives a fixed amount of money at predetermined times, often at regularly scheduled intervals.

▶ **GRIT** – Grantor-retained incomes trust designates specific people to receive certain property, such as stocks or a house, but the income or use of the property stays with you until your death.

▶ **GRUT** – Grantor-retained unit trust pays a specific percentage to the beneficiary.

Gross Estate – The value of all property owned by the deceased person on the date of that person's death; this is what gets taxed.

Guardian – The person legally appointed to be responsible for the needs of minor children until they reach a legal age; also, any adult who can be legally appointed to manage the affairs of an incompetent or infirmed adult of any age.

Guardianship Clause – The appointment of a guardian for minor children (under the age of 18); a successor guardian should also be named as a backup.

H

Health Care Power of Attorney – Also known as medical power of attorney, this is the designation of a person who makes medical decisions for you when you cannot do it for yourself.

Heir – The legal title of a person who inherits property from an estate that does not have a will, or is intestate; beneficiaries are those who receive an inheritance by being named in a legal document, such as a will or trust.

Holographic Will – This is a handwritten document signed by you but not witnessed by anyone else. Some states recognize a handwritten will as valid; others do not, so you need to check your state laws if you want to use this kind of will. New Jersey recognizes holographic wills.

Homeowner's Insurance – The exchange of premiums for a guaranteed payment to cover the loss of a house and other personal property in the residence. Other coverage can also be included, such as personal liability.

Homestead Exemption Statute – State law that protects a family home from being sold to pay off creditors if there is not enough money in an estate to cover outstanding debt.

I

Individual Retirement Arrangement (IRA) – An investment account that you set up for yourself for retirement savings. There is a limit to the contributions you can make annually. There is a tax deduction for making these contributions every year, so technically they are tax-free contributions.

▶ **Roth IRA** – Named after its primary legislative sponsor, Senator William Roth of Delaware. Contributions to this IRA are also tax-deductible in the year they are made, and taxes are paid when the money is withdrawn. The difference here is that the interest earned while the money is invested will be tax-free if you own the Roth IRA for at least five years.

Inheritance Tax – A state tax levied on the property received by a beneficiary.

Insurance – A method of protecting valuables in the form of a policy in which premiums are paid over time to guarantee a specific payment for a specific purpose by the company accepting the premiums. Those valuables can be property, such as your home, car, or jewelry; a person; the ability to work and care for yourself; life; health care; and long-term care.

Insurance Agent – An individual who is authorized by an insurance company to represent that company when dealing with an applicant for insurance, be it a medical, disability, dental, or long-term care policy. An agent can help you with your policy purchase by assessing the kind and amount of insurance you need and can afford.

Intestate – To die without a will.

Inter vivos Trust – A trust that is set up and takes effect during your lifetime, before your death.

Irrevocable – A trust that cannot be changed, no matter what.

Joint Will – This is one legal document for any two people, such as you and your spouse. The problem with this kind of will is that it is irrevocable, which means it cannot be changed after one of the two parties dies. The reason is that all decisions must be made by both people. A lawyer can tell you when this kind of will is a good idea, but most suggest separate wills to avoid complications.

Joint-with-survivor Pension – When an employee dies, his or her benefits will be paid to his or her spouse for the remainder of the spouse's life. If the spouse waives that right, then the employee's pension payments will be larger (no need to set aside extra money for future payments), and the pension payments end when the employee dies.

K

Keogh Plan – Pronounced "key-oh," this is a qualified retirement plan for sole proprietors and partners but also can be used by employees. The restrictions, distributions, and other details are similar to a defined contribution plan or defined benefit plan.

"Kiddie Tax" – The nickname used to describe an income tax applied to money that minors did not earn through employment, also called unearned income. The special laws passed in 1996 were created to close a loophole that allowed parents to give their children a large gift as a way to pay a lower tax on the interest earned; the child tax rate was significantly lower than the adult rate.

L

Lawyer – An individual who has completed a course of study in the law and passed a state certification exam that authorizes him or her to practice law and/or give legal advice. Also called attorneys, these people can specialize in specific aspects of estate planning, such as wills, trusts, or probate court, or they might have a more broad focus, such as estate planning or tax law.

Legal Title – Legal position that gives the trustee ownership of the property in a trust for the duration of the trustee's responsibility.

Liability – A debt or an obligation to pay money to another person or institution.

Life Insurance – A financial arrangement in which an individual makes payments on a policy that guarantees the payment of a specific amount of money to a beneficiary upon the death of the person who is covered by the policy.

Living Trust – Created while you are still alive, this trust allows you to be the grantor, trustee, and beneficiary if you choose; this is considered a will substitute as a way to avoid probate.

Living Will – Also known as a medical directive, this is a legal document in which you spell out the decisions you have made about your medical care while you are still alive.

Long-term Care Insurance – This insurance provides payments to cover the cost of medical care. In-home nursing or nursing home fees are examples of what might be covered.

M

Marital Dedication Trust – Puts property into a trust that is exclusively for your spouse, who decides what happens to the property after your death.

Medical Insurance – Frequently referred to as health insurance by those who sell it, the insurance that covers medical costs when you are sick and trying to cure an illness, injured, pregnant, and for regular checkups.

Medicaid – State-run medical insurance plan that is supported by federal funding and provides medical benefits that are minimal for the financially needy. To qualify for this plan, you have to possess no more than a set dollar amount in property.

Medicare – A medical insurance program offered by the federal government to people who are 65 or older, certain disabled people under the age of 65, and anyone with permanent kidney failure.

▶ Part A of this coverage is hospital insurance and Part B is medical insurance. Part B now comes with a monthly premium.

Medical Power of Attorney – Also known as health care power of attorney, this is the designation of a person who makes medical decisions for you when you cannot do it for yourself.

Minor Trust – A way to give gifts to a minor that avoids the gift tax and keeps the property safe until the minor becomes an adult and can take ownership of the trust.

Marital Trust – A trust for the surviving legal spouse of the deceased.

Mutual Will – A plan for your estate that is prepared in conjunction with another person.

N

Net Worth – A person's true financial value: Assets – Liabilities = Net Worth.

Noncharitable Trust – A trust that has a person or institution that is not a charity as the beneficiary.

Nonstatutory Living Will – A legal document in which you spell out the decisions you have made about your medical care while you are still alive that does not comply with the laws of your state. A statutory document will likely provide more protection for the physicians and nurses carrying out your wishes.

Nuncupative Will – Also called an oral will, this is a spoken will. Some states only allow this kind of will if someone is literally on their deathbed, and it only covers personal property of little or no value. Again, you need to check with your state on the laws regarding this kind of will. New Jersey does not recognize nuncupative wills.

O

Opening Clauses – Lay out the basic information about who you are and set the stage for the clauses that follow. The introductory clause identifies you as the person who is making the will, the family statement clause introduces and identifies the family members who will be referred to later in the will, and the tax clause explains how the taxes on your estate will be paid.

Outright Charitable Gift – This is property you give to a charity and get nothing in return for; the gift can be cash or any other type of property.

Ownership – The individual(s) who hold the legal title to a piece of property; the ability to retain, sell, or give away this property depends on the number of people who hold that title, in some cases, their relationship, and any legal agreements/contracts connected to the property.

▶ **Sole Ownership** – A single person holds the title to the property.

▶ **Joint Ownership** – When any two people hold an equal share of the title to a piece of property; the most common form is spousal, or when a legally married couple has both names on a title to a piece of property.

▶ **Community Property** – A state law that views a wife and husband as equal partners and assumes a 50/50 split of ownership. Applies in Arizona, California, Idaho, Louisiana, Nevada, New Mexico, Texas, Washington, and Wisconsin.

▶ **Separate Property** – Things owned by one spouse that are not part of the couple's community property.

▶ **Joint Tenancy** – A group of people who hold an equal and undivided title to a piece of property.

P

Payable-on-Death (POD) – An account, like a savings account, that has a specific stipulation that the death of the original owner automatically transfers the ownership to a named beneficiary.

Pension Benefit Guarantee Corporation (PBGC) – A federal agency that can insure and therefore protect some or all of your pension if your plan qualifies for the coverage and your company purchases the insurance.

Pension Plan – A program that is set up by an employer, including government agencies, to pay employees benefits upon retirement. Each employee has an individual account, and the employer makes a contribution to each employee's account based on the terms of the plan. There are two common types of pension plans.

▶ **Defined Benefit Plan** – A plan in which the employee will receive a specified amount of money upon retirement; the amount of the disbursement made is based on the number of years of employment.

▶ **Defined Contribution Plan** – A pension plan that sets a specific amount an employee will put into the plan (a percentage of income) and makes payments only for the amount of money contributed to the plan.

Phishing – The act of fraudulently representing an e-mail, website pop-up window, or other electronic communication as being from a bank, some other financial institution, or a legitimate business that requests the verification of personal information. These communications also request "missing" information and updates to intentionally incorrect data.

Pourover Will – This places some property into a trust that was established while you were still alive.

Probate Court – The state-level court system that is specifically set up to handle all matters related to the distribution of a deceased person's estate; this is where a will is filed and unanswered questions about the disbursement of an estate are settled by a judge.

Profit-sharing Plan – Employees receive a portion of the profits earned by the company; the plan determines the amount that will be contributed to each employee's account.

Property – Also referred to as personal property, this comprises your possessions. This category is further divided into:

▶ **Real Property** – Any kind of real estate, such as a house, a condo, or a vacant lot.

▶ **Tangible Personal Property** – The things you can touch, such as a signed baseball, jewelry, or linen bed sheets.

▶ **Intangible Personal Property** – Checking accounts, savings accounts, money market funds, mutual funds, stocks, bonds, or retirement accounts, such as a pension, an IRA, a Roth IRA, or a Keogh plan.

Property Guardian – Also known as a property manager, this is a legal adult who takes responsibility for the oversight of property inherited by a minor/child. Children under the age of 18 can inherit property, but they can only be allowed to legally own that property with adult supervision; an adult must have the responsibility of managing it.

Property Interest – This refers to the connection a person has to a specific item, piece of land, or other items.

▶ **Legal Interest** – This is property that a person can legally transfer or manage, but it is not owned by the individual. Someone who is responsible for the maintenance and oversight of the use of a piece of property but who does not legally own it is called a trustee.

▶ **Beneficial Interest** – You receive a benefit from the property.

Protective Trusts – These trusts are designed with conditions to protect the beneficiary's property.

Provisions – Clauses that explain how you want your wishes carried out.

Q

QTIP – A qualified terminable interest property trust is a marital deduction trust, but instead of your spouse deciding who gets the property after your death, the grantor makes that decision.

Qualified Pension Plan – A plan in which the amount of money that the employer puts into an employee's account is not taxed as income during the fiscal year the contribution is made.

R

Renter's Insurance – The exchange of premiums for a guaranteed payment to cover the loss of personal property housed in rental property that is used as a primary residence.

Revocable – A trust that can be changed.

S

Simple Will – A legal document that identifies whom you are, your beneficiaries, your executor, the directions you leave for the care of people for whom you are responsible, and the distribution of your assets.

Skimming – The act of using a special high-tech storage device to electronically "grab" account numbers and other information from a store computer register when a credit card transaction/purchase is processing.

Social Security Disability Benefit – Monthly payment made by the federal government to qualified recipients who can no longer work. Payments are made until the age of 65; at that point, recipients begin to receive the social security retirement benefit at the same rate.

Social Security Retirement Benefit – Monthly payment made by the federal government to qualified recipients who reach retirement age. Payments are based on contributions made during the individual's employment period.

Social Security Supplemental Security Income (SSI) – The federal government makes a monthly payment to qualified individuals. This benefit is for people who have little (if any) property or are blind or disabled in some other way.

Special Needs Trust – A support trust for a disabled person under the age of 65 (you or anyone else). This trust makes payments on the beneficiaries' behalf, as required by the state as reimbursement. After the beneficiary dies, the property in the trust is paid to other beneficiaries. This trust is designed to protect your property from seizure by the government or a creditor seeking reimbursement.

Special Provisions – Encompasses all clauses that create specific requirements that are unique to the beneficiary or the assets. For example, a beneficiary of a trust might be required to be 21 or graduate college before he or she can take ownership of that trust.

Spendthrift Trust – A trust set up for someone who will be unable to handle his or her own affairs, who is mentally incompetent, or who might have financial problems and needs protection from creditors. The beneficiary does not own the property in the trust, just the payments that are made from the trust.

Spiritual Advisor – A minister, priest, monk, or some other cleric or individual trained in a specific faith tradition who offers guidance, support, and information related to their belief system.

Split-interest Trust – More than one individual benefits from the trust. One person or charity would have an interest in the trust for a specific period of time, and then another person or charity receives the property that remains.

State Estate Tax – A tax levied by the state on property left in an estate after a person dies, similar to the estate tax by the federal government, but the state tax is an additional tax burden. Not all states have an estate tax; New Jersey does.

State Gift Tax – A tax by individual states according to terms they set that are levied against any property you give to another person or institution during a fiscal year; it can be in cash or the transfer of property, such as real estate or jewelry. Many of these taxes are tied in some way to the federal estate tax.

State Income Tax – A tax on income earned during a fiscal year that is for residents of that state. Income earned in another state might be taxable in your state of residence, and any inheritance you receive that counts as income and is entered on your federal tax form also can be taxed.

Statutory Living Will – A legal document in which you spell out the decisions you have made about your medical care while you are still alive that complies with the statutes or laws of your state. A statutory document will likely provide more protection than a nonstatutory living will for the physicians and nurses carrying out your wishes.

Stock Bailout – The transfer of stock ownership from your name to that of a charity; the fair market value of the stock at the time of the transfer is the gift amount.

Stock Bonus Plan – A retirement plan established by an employer to give shares of the company's stock to employees. When the employee receives the shares, he or she must pay taxes based on the value of the stock.

▶ **Employee Stock Ownership Plan (ESOP)** – A retirement type of stock bonus plan. The employer contributes shares of its stock to a qualified trust, and the employee only pays taxes based on distributions he or she receives.

Successor Trustee – Someone who will step in if the primary trustee is unable to serve or cannot continue to manage your trust. This person will have the same legal obligations for managing the trust as the original trustee should the successor assume the management responsibilities.

Supplemental Needs Trust – A support trust for a handicapped, elderly, or disabled person in need of support is assisted by this trust in such a way that it does not reduce or jeopardize the eligibility of that person to receive public or private benefits. This trust is designed to protect your property from seizure by the government or a creditor seeking reimbursement.

Support Trust – Requires a trustee to pay only the income and property necessary to cover the cost of education or assistance, such as health care fees or nursing home fees of the beneficiaries.

Survival Clause – This leaves everything in your estate to one named person. Married people frequently do this to ensure that everything goes to the surviving spouse.

Survivor Benefit – A portion of the deceased employee's pension paid to the surviving spouse. The amount, regularly a percentage, is set by the terms of the pension plan rules.

T

Tax-deferred – The taxes on money put into an investment account are paid when it is received by the employee in the form of a distribution, not at the time the money goes into the account.

Term Insurance – A life insurance policy that carries an annual premium and pays a specified death benefit to the beneficiary but does not have a cash value, so you cannot borrow money from it. The only payment made is to the beneficiary. The death benefit is not paid if premium payments stop.

▶ **Annual Renewable** – A term life policy that has an annual premium and can be renewed from year to year; be sure you understand the renewal rights before signing.

▶ **Decreasing** – A term life policy in which premiums remain the same, but the benefit decreases over time. For example, if you purchase this kind of insurance (also called mortgage or credit term insurance) to pay off your debts after you die, the mortgage you want to insure might be $250,000 at the time you purchase the insurance, but the mortgage value when you die might be $150,000. The policy then pays $150,000. This kind of insurance is recommended only for those who cannot get any other kind of insurance.

▶ **Level** – A term life policy with coverage that is guaranteed for a specific period of time, or term, such as five, ten, or 20 years at a specific premium. The premium will remain for the five-year period, but at year six, it will go up and remain at that rate through the tenth year, continuing after that.

▶ **Group** – Employers frequently purchase a term life policy for each employee as an added benefit. Employees get an excellent low rate, and there is no income tax on the premiums for the first $50,000 of coverage.

Testamentary Trust – A fund created by the terms of your will after your death.

Testamentary Trust Will – This will moves your assets into one or more trusts after your death.

Testator – A person who writes a will.

Totten Trust – This is a bank account that upon your death immediately passes to the named beneficiary.

Trust – A legal arrangement that involves the transfer of property from the original owner to a person or a company for the purpose of holding and maintaining the property for the benefit of a specific individual, group of people, or institution(s).

Trustee – The person or company that will oversee or manage a financial resources account, such as a trust or custodial account, once it is established. This person or group will make sure the property in the trust is safe and in good order until it is turned over to the beneficiary.

Trust Agreement – The legal document that spells out the terms of a trust, including the people and conditions and the rules that must be followed; some terms are state or federal laws, and other terms are specific conditions.

Trustor – The person who sets up the trust. Other names commonly used are creator, donor, settlor, or grantor.

Trust Principal – The name given to property that is placed into a trust and is managed by a trust agreement.

U

Umbrella Liability Insurance – The exchange of premiums for a guaranteed payment to cover a host of situations that would put personal property at risk, such as personal liability or negligence.

V

Vested – To meet the predetermined requirements contained within a pension plan based on the number of years you have worked for the employer.

Before an employee can receive any distributions or take full ownership of a pension plan, the employee must be fully vested.

W

Waiver – A written statement declining the right to receive benefits signed by a spouse. This waiver must be signed to legally sever the right to claim any benefits — an alternative agreement, such as signing a prenuptial agreement, will not be enough.

Whole Life Insurance – Sometimes called cash value life insurance, this is a form of life insurance for which the insured person pays a monthly or annual premium to a company that will, upon the owner's death, pay a predetermined, fixed amount of money to the beneficiaries. A portion of the fixed (meaning it will never go up or down) premium is invested, another portion is placed into an account, like a savings account, and that cash value is accessible to the policy owner. It can be borrowed against as a loan, or the cash can be taken as the proceeds of the policy instead of the death benefit payout.

► **Universal Life** – A kind of whole life policy that guarantees a minimum return, but the value of the policy can go up or down. If the policy makes more money, the return might be high enough to cover your premium payments.

► **Joint First-to-Die or Second-to-Die** – Just as it sounds, this is a policy held by two people, and the beneficiary is paid after the first or second person dies, as designated in the policy.

Will – A legal document in which you identify what people or institutions will receive money and property from your estate after your death; it also serves to appoint guardianship of children or adults who are your legal responsibility and designates an executor to manage your estate after you die.

Will Substitute – An agreement, contract, or other legal arrangement that will accomplish the same goals of a will — to protect and transfer property rights — but without the use of a will document.

APPENDIX C

New Jersey Advance Directive Forms

This chapter contains forms to help you prepare in advance for important health care decisions. Included is New Jersey's Instructive Directive form, which will let you have a say in your future medical care. It will also spell out in advance what medical treatments you wish to accept or refuse and the circumstances in which you want your wishes implemented. The second form is a Proxy Directive for New Jersey, which lets you designate a person (proxy) you trust and give that person legal authority for future medical care if you are unable to make decisions for yourself.

The New Jersey Commission on Legal and Ethical Problems in the Delivery of Health Care

INSTRUCTION DIRECTIVE

I understand that as a competent adult I have the right to make decisions about my health care. There may come a time when I am unable, due to physical or mental incapacity, to make my own health care decisions. In these circumstances, those caring for me will need direction concerning my care and they will require information about my values and health care wishes. In order to provide the guidance and authority needed to make decisions on my behalf:

A) I, _____, hereby declare and make known to my family, physician, and others, my instructions and wishes for my future health care. I direct that all health care decisions, including decisions to accept or refuse any treatment, service or procedure used to diagnose, treat or care for my physical or mental condition and decisions to provide, withhold or withdraw life-sustaining measures, be made in accordance with my wishes as expressed in this document. This instruction directive shall take effect in the event I become unable to make my own health care decisions, as determined by the physician who has primary responsibility for my care, and any necessary confirming determinations. I direct that this document become part of my permanent medical records.

Part One: Statement of My Wishes Concerning My Future Health Care

*In **Part One**, you are asked to provide instructions concerning your future health care. This will require making important and perhaps difficult choices. Before completing your directive, you should discuss these matters with your doctor, family members or others who may become responsible for your care.*

*In **Section B and C**, you may state the circumstances in which various forms of medical treatment, including life-sustaining measures, should be provided, withheld or discontinued. If the options and choices below do not fully express your wishes, you should use **Section D**, and/or attach a statement to this document which would provide those responsible for your care with additional information you think would help them in making decisions about your medical treatment. **Please familiarize yourself with all sections of Part One before completing your directive**.*

B) GENERAL INSTRUCTIONS: To inform those responsible for my care of my specific wishes, I make the following statement of personal views regarding my health care:

Initial ONE of the following two statements with which you agree:

1. _____ I direct that all medically appropriate measures be provided to sustain my life, regardless of my physical or mental condition

2. _____ There are circumstances in which I would not want my life to be prolonged by further medical treatment. In these circumstances, life-sustaining measures should not be initiated and if they have been, they should be discontinued. I recognize that this is likely to hasten my death. In the following, I specify the circumstances in which I would choose to forego life-sustaining measures.

The New Jersey Commission on Legal and Ethical Problems in the Delivery of Health Care

If you have initialed statement 2 on page 1, please initial each of the statements (a, b, c) with which you agree:

a. _____ I realize that there may come a time when I am diagnosed as having an incurable and irreversible illness, disease, or condition. If this occurs, and my attending physician and at least one additional physician who has personally examined me determine that my condition is **terminal**, I direct that life-sustaining measures which would serve only to artificially prolong my dying be withheld or discontinued. I also direct that I be given all medically appropriate care necessary to make me comfortable and to relieve pain.

In the space provided, write in the bracketed phrase with which you agree:

To me, terminal condition means that my physicians have determined that:

_____

[**I will die within a few days**] [**I will die within a few weeks**]
[**I have a life expectancy of approximately** _____ **or less** *(enter 6 months, or 1 year)*]

b. _____ If there should come a time when I come **permanently unconscious**, and it is determined by my attending physician and at least one additional physician with appropriate expertise who has personally examined me, that I have totally and irreversibly lost consciousness and my capacity for interaction with other people and my surroundings, I direct that life-sustaining measures be withheld or discontinued. I understand that I will not experience pain or discomfort in this condition, and I direct that I be given all my medically appropriate care necessary to provide for my personal hygiene and dignity.

c. _____ I realize that there may come a time when I am diagnosed as having an **incurable and irreversible** illness, disease, or condition which may not be terminal. My condition may cause me to experience severe and progressive physical or mental deterioration and/or a permanent loss of capacities and faculties I value highly. If, in the course of my medical care, the burdens of continued life with treatment become greater than the benefits I experience, I direct that life-sustaining measures be withheld or discontinued. I also direct that I be given all medically appropriate care necessary to make me comfortable and to relieve pain.

*(Paragraph c. covers a wide range of possible situations in which you may have experienced partial or complete loss of certain mental and physical capacities you value highly. If you wish, in the space provided below you may specify in more detail the conditions in which you would choose to forego life-sustaining measures. You might include a description of the faculties or capacities, which, if irretrievably lost would lead you to accept death rather than continue living. You may want to express any special concerns you have about particular medical conditions or treatments, or any other considerations which would provide further guidance to those who may become responsible for your care. If necessary, you may attach a separate statement to this document or use **Section D** to provide additional instructions.)*

Examples of conditions which I find unacceptable are:

_____
_____
_____
_____

The New Jersey Commission on Legal and Ethical Problems in the Delivery of Health Care

C) SPECIFIC INSTRUCTIONS: **Artificially Provided Fluids and Nutrition; Cardiopulmonary Resuscitation (CPR).** *On page 2 you provided general instructions regarding life-sustaining measures. Here you are asked to give specific instructions regarding two types of life-sustaining measures-artificially provided fluids and nutrition and cardiopulmonary resuscitation.*

In the space provided, write in the bracketed phrase with which you agree:

1. In the circumstances I initialed on page 2, I also direct that artificially provided fluids and nutrition, such as by feeding tube or intravenous infusion,

_____

[be withheld or withdrawn and that I be allowed to die]
[be provided to the extent medically appropriate]

2. In the circumstances I initialed on page 2, if I should suffer a cardiac arrest, I also direct that cardiopulmonary resuscitation (CPR)

_____

[not be provided and that I be allowed to die]
[be provided to preserve my life, unless medically inappropriate or futile]

3. If neither of the above statements adequately expresses your wishes concerning artificially provided fluids and nutrition or CPR, please explain your wishes below.

_____

_____

_____

D) ADDITIONAL INSTRUCTIONS: *(You should provide any additional information about your health care preferences which is important to you and which may help those concerned with your care to implement your wishes. You may wish to direct your family members or your health care providers to consult with others, or you may wish to direct that your care be provided by a particular physician, hospital, nursing home, or at home. If you are or believe you may become pregnant, you may wish to state specific instructions. If you need more space than is provided here you may attach an additional statement to this directive.)*

_____

_____

_____

E) BRAIN DEATH: *(The State of New Jersey recognizes the irreversible cessation of all functions of the entire brain, including the brain stem (also known as whole brain death), as a legal standard for the declaration of death. However, individuals who cannot accept this standard because of their personal religious beliefs may request that it not be applied in determining their death.)*

Initial the following statement only if it applies to you:

_____ To declare my death on the basis of the whole brain death standard would violate my personal religious beliefs. I therefore wish my death to be declared solely on the basis of the traditional criteria of irreversible cessation of cardiopulmonary (heartbeat and breathing) function.

F) AFTER DEATH - ANATOMICAL GIFTS: *(It is now possible to transplant human organs and tissue in order to save and improve the lives of others. Organs, tissues and other body parts are also used for therapy, medical research and education. This section allows you to indicate your desire to make an anatomical gift and if so, to provide instructions for any limitations or special uses.)*

Initial the statements which express your wishes:

1. _____ **I wish** to make the following anatomical gift to take effect upon my death:

    A. _____ any needed organs or body parts

    B. _____ only the following organs or parts

    _____

for the purposes of transplantation, therapy, medical research or education, or

    C. _____ my body for anatomical study, if needed.

    D. _____ special limitations, if any:

    _____

If you wish to provide additional instructions, such as indicating your preference that your organs be given to a specific person or institution, or be used for a specific purpose, please do so in the space provided below.

_____
_____
_____

2. _____ **I do not wish** to make an anatomical gift upon my death.

Part Two: Signature and Witnesses

G) COPIES: The original or a copy of this document has been given to the following people *(NOTE: It is important that you provide a family member, friend or your physician with a copy of your directive.):*

1. *name* _____   2. *name* _____

   address _____   *address* _____

   city _____ *state* _____   *city* _____ *state* _____

   telephone _____   *telephone* _____

The New Jersey Commission on Legal and Ethical Problems in the Delivery of Health Care

H) SIGNATURE: By writing this advance directive, I inform those who may become entrusted with my health care of my wishes and intend to ease the burdens of decision making which this responsibility may impose. I understand the purpose and effect of this document and sign it knowingly, voluntarily and after careful deliberation.

Signed this _____ **day of** _____, 20_____.

signature _____

address _____

city _____ *state*_____

I) WITNESSES: I declare that the person who signed this document, or asked another to sign this document on his or her behalf, did so in my presence, that he or she is personally known to me and that he or she appears to be of sound mind and free of duress or undue influence. I am 18 years of age or older, and am not designated by this or any other document as the person's health care representative nor as an alternate health care representative.

1. *witness* _____

   address _____

   city _____ *state* _____

   signature _____

   date _____

2. *witness* _____

   address _____

   city _____ *state* _____

   signature _____

   date _____

The New Jersey Commission on Legal and Ethical Problems in the Delivery of Health Care

PROXY DIRECTIVE--(Durable Power of Attorney for Health Care)
Designation of Health Care Representative

I understand that as a competent adult, I have the right to make decisions about my health care. There may come a time when I am unable, due to physical or mental incapacity, to make my own health care decision. In these circumstances, those caring for me will need direction and they will turn to someone who knows my values and health care wishes. By writing this durable power of attorney for health care I appoint a health care representative with the legal authority to make health care decisions on my behalf and to consult with my physician and others. I direct that this document become part of my permanent medical records.

A) CHOOSING A HEALTH CARE REPRESENTATIVE:

I, _____, hereby designate _____,

of _____

_____,

(home address and telephone number of health care representative)

as my health care representative to make any and all health care decisions for me, including decisions to accept or to refuse any treatment, service or procedure used to diagnose or treat my physical or mental condition and decisions to provide, withhold or withdraw life-sustaining measures. I direct my representative to make decisions on my behalf in accordance with my wishes as stated in this document, or as otherwise known to him or her. In the event my wishes are not clear, my representative is authorized to make decisions in my best interest, based on what is known of my wishes.

This durable power of attorney for health care shall take effect in the event I become unable to make my own health care decisions, as determined by the physician who has primary responsibility for my care, and any necessary confirming determinations.

B) ALTERNATE REPRESENTATIVES: If the person I have designated above is unable, unwilling or unavailable to act as my health care representative, I hereby designate the following person(s) to act as my health care representative, in the order of priority stated:

1. *name* _____   2. *name* _____

   address _____   *address* _____

   city _____ *state* _____   *city* _____ *state* _____

   telephone _____   *telephone* _____

C) SPECIFIC DIRECTIONS: Please initial the statement below which best expresses your wishes.

_____ My health care representative is authorized to direct that artificially provided fluids and nutrition, such as by feeding tube or intravenous infusion, be withheld or withdrawn.

_____ My health care representative does not have this authority, and I direct that artificially provided fluids and nutrition be provided to preserve my life, to the extent medically appropriate.

Page 1 of 2

The New Jersey Commission on Legal and Ethical Problems in the Delivery of Health Care

(If you have any additional specific instructions concerning your care you may use the space below or attach an additional statement.)

_____

_____

_____

_____

D) COPIES: The original or a copy of this document has been given to my health care representative and to the following:

1. name _____

    address _____

    city _____ state _____   telephone _____

2. name _____

    address _____

    city _____ state _____   telephone _____

E) SIGNATURE: By writing this durable power of attorney for health care, I inform those who may become entrusted with my care of my health care wishes and intend to ease the burdens of decision making which this responsibility may impose. I have discussed the terms of this designation with my health care representative and he or she has willingly agreed to accept the responsibility for acting on my behalf in accordance with my wishes as expressed in this document. I understand the purpose and effect of this document and sign it knowingly, voluntarily and after careful deliberation.

Signed this _____ **day of** _____, 20_____.

signature _____

address _____

city _____ state_____

F) WITNESSES: I declare that the person who signed this document, or asked another to sign this document on his or her behalf, did so in my presence, that he or she is personally known to me, and that he or she appears to be of sound mind and free of duress or undue influence. I am 18 years of age or older, and am not designated by this or any other document as the person's health care representative, nor as an alternate health care representative.

1. witness_____   2. witness _____

    address _____   address _____

    city _____ state _____   city _____ state _____

    signature _____   signature _____

    date _____   date _____

BIBLIOGRAPHY

"Gift Tax." Internal Revenue Service. **www.irs.gov/businesses/small/ article/0,,id=164872,00.html.** Accessed on January 26, 2010.

Jurkovic, Daniel. (2007, April 5). "The New Guardianship Law Spina Bifida Association Tri-State Region Teleconference." Rutherford, NJ. **www.thesbrn.org/wp-content/uploads/2009/06/LimitedGuardianshi-pLawSummaryDJJ_001.pdf.** Accessed on September 30, 2010.

Hagan, Kevin. (2008, July 2). "New Jersey Inheritance Tax." **www.asso-ciatedcontent.com/article/828271/new_jersey_inheritance_tax.html.** Accessed on October 1, 2010.

"Instruction Directive." (n.d.) The New Jersey Commission on Legal and Ethical Problems in the Delivery of Health Care. State of New Jersey Department of Health and Senior Services. **http://nj.gov/health/advancedirective/documents/instruction_directive.pdf.** Accessed on October 1, 2010.

"Majority of American Adults Remain without Wills New Lawyers.com Survey Finds." Harris Interactive. **www.harrisinteractive.com/news/news-letters/clientnews/2007_Lawyers.pdf.** Accessed on January 26, 2010.

New Jersey Annotated Statutes

"New Jersey Estate Tax – Important Provisions and Filing Requirements." (2010). State of New Jersey Department of Treasury. **www.state.nj.us/ treasury/taxation/revesttax.shtml.** Accessed on October 1, 2010.

"New Jersey Medicaid Program Eligibility." (2009.) **www.state.nj.us/ humanservices/dmahs/clients/medicaid/medicaid_program_ eligibility.pdf.** Accessed October 1, 2010.

"Proxy Directive – (Durable Power of Attorney for Health Care)." (n.d.) The New Jersey Commission on Legal and Ethical Problems in the Delivery of Health Care. The State of New Jersey Department of Health and Senior Services. **http://nj.gov/health/advancedirective/documents/ proxy_directive.pdf.** Accessed on October 1, 2010.

Reinhart, Christopher. (2008, February 6.) "Murder and Inheritance." **www. cga.ct.gov/2008/rpt/2008-R-0086.htm.** Accessed on October 1, 2010.

Rubenstein, Joshua S. (2007). "Standby Guardianship Legislation: at the Midway Point." ACTEC Journal 33:1, p. 2. **www.actec.org/resources/ publications/notes/PDFNotes/ACTECJournal-Summer2007.pdf.** Accessed on October 4, 2010

"Standby Guardianship: Summary of State Laws." (2008.) Child Welfare Information Gateway. **www.childwelfare.gov/systemwide/laws_policies/ statutes/guardianshipall.pdf.** Accessed on October 1, 2010.

"Surrogate Taxes." (2010). Middlesex County, NJ. **www.co.middlesex. nj.us/surrogate/taxes.asp.** Accessed on October 2, 2010.

"UTMA/UGMA Custodial Accounts." (2008). **http://yillionaire.com/ utma_ugma.aspx.** Accessed on October 3, 2010.

U.S. Department of Labor. Bureau of Labor Statistics. **www.bls.gov.** Accessed on January 26, 2010.

INDEX

Mount Laurel Library
100 Walt Whitman Avenue